FAVORITE NOVENAS AND PRAYERS

Favorite Novenas
and
Prayers

compiled and edited
by
Norma Cronin Cassidy

PAULIST® PRESS
New York / Paramus / Toronto

NIHIL OBSTAT:
Rev. Charles W. Gusmer
Censor Librorum

IMPRIMATUR:
✝ Thomas A. Boland
Archbishop of Newark

September 29, 1972

Library of Congress
Catalog Card Number: 72-91456

ISBN 0-8091-1761-4

Published by Paulist Press
Editorial Office: 1865 Broadway, N.Y., N.Y. 10023
Business Office: 400 Sette Drive, Paramus, N.J. 07652

Printed and bound in the
United States of America

Contents

GENERAL PRAYERS

Foreword

When at the Last Supper Christ gave himself to his Apostles under the form of bread and wine, there took place the identification He talked about in the sixth chapter of St. John. "He that eateth my flesh and drinketh my blood abideth in me and I in him." This identification went in two directions: the Apostles acquired a new family background in the life of God; Christ took upon himself the iniquity of us all.

Since the family life of God and the sinful life of the family of men are incompatible, one had to go.

So Christ died on the Cross, taking down with him into the ground the sin which touched his sinlessness in the Eucharistic identification. The Apostles, and all of us, died with him. So did sin lose its hold on us.

When Our Lord, and we with him, rose from the dead the new family background of the re-deemed was the same as that of God's own Son. We live now and operate as one who has his roots in heaven.

The resurrection is the visibility of all this.

There have been many resurrections since that first on Easter morning. One of them is this little collection of novenas and prayers which Norma Cassidy has collected for us in the present volume.

With all that has happened since Vatican II many things long associated with devotions and liturgy in the Church have died; their defects or shortcomings, their out-of-dateness dying with them. There was nothing wrong with them (no sin in them) save their inability to weather the way of the Cross which the Church has been going through, to die to a life which was of the past, so as to live in a growing world still to be redeemed.

These novenas and prayers have now risen from the dead. They come to us with the vigor of a resurrection because all that is in them is imperishable, and full of the life of heaven. Only the best survive.

Thomas H. Moore, S.J.

Daily
Prayers

The Our Father

Our Father, who art in heaven, hallowed be Thy name; Thy kingdom come; Thy will be done on earth as it is in heaven. Give us this day our daily bread; and forgive us our trespasses as we forgive those who trespass against us; and lead us not into temptation, but deliver us from evil.   Amen.

The Hail Mary

Hail, Mary, full of grace! the Lord is with thee; blessed art thou among women, and blessed is the fruit of thy womb, Jesus. Holy Mary, Mother of God, pray for us sinners, now and at the hour of our death.   Amen.

The Apostles' Creed

I believe in God, the Father Almighty, Creator of heaven and earth; and in Jesus Christ, His only Son, our Lord; who was conceived by the

3

Holy Spirit, born of the Virgin Mary, suffered under Pontius Pilate; was crucified; died and was buried. He descended into hell; the third day He arose again from the dead; He ascended into heaven, sits at the right hand of God, the Father Almighty; from thence He shall come to judge the living and the dead. I believe in the Holy Spirit, the holy Catholic Church, the communion of Saints, the forgiveness of sins, the resurrection of the body, and life everlasting.   Amen.

The Confiteor

I confess to Almighty God, to blessed Mary, ever Virgin, to blessed Michael the Archangel, to blessed John the Baptist, to the holy Apostles Peter and Paul, and to all the Saints, that I have sinned exceedingly in thought, word and deed, through my fault, through my fault, through my most grievous fault. Therefore I beseech blessed Mary, ever Virgin, blessed Michael the Archangel, blessed John the Baptist, the holy Apostles Peter and Paul, and all the Saints, to pray to the Lord our God for me.

May the Almighty God have mercy on me, and forgive me my sins, and bring me to everlasting life.   Amen.

May the Almighty and merciful Lord grant me pardon, absolution, and remission of all my sins. Amen.

Act of Faith

O my God, I firmly believe that Thou art one God in three Divine Persons, Father, Son and Holy Spirit; I believe that Thy Divine Son became man, and died for our sins, and that He will come to judge the living and the dead. I believe these and all the truths which the holy Catholic Church teaches because Thou hast revealed them, who can neither deceive nor be deceived.

Act of Hope

O my God, relying on Thy infinite goodness and promises, I hope to obtain pardon of my sins, the help of Thy grace and life everlasting, through the merits of Jesus Christ, my Lord and Redeemer.

Act of Love

O my God, I love Thee above all things, with my whole heart and soul, because Thou art all-good and worthy of all love. I love my neighbor as myself for love of Thee. I forgive all who have injured me and ask pardon of all whom I have injured.

Act of Contrition

O my God, I am heartily sorry for having offended Thee and I detest all my sins because I dread the loss of heaven and the pains of hell, but most of all because they offend Thee, my God, who art all good and deserving of all my love. I firmly resolve with the help of Thy grace, to confess my sins, to do penance and to amend my life.   Amen.

The Memorare

Remember, O most gracious Virgin Mary, that never was it known that anyone who fled to thy protection, implored thy help and sought thy intercession, was left unaided. Inspired with this confidence, I fly unto thee, O Virgin of virgins, my mother! To thee I come, before thee I stand sinful and sorrowful. O Mother of the Word Incarnate, despise not my petitions, but in thy mercy hear and answer me.   Amen.

Prayer to St. Michael

Saint Michael, the Archangel, defend us in battle; be our protection against the malice and snares of the devil. We humbly beseech Thee, O God, to command him; and do thou, O prince of the heavenly host, by the divine power, thrust into hell Satan and the other evil spirits who roam through the world seeking the destruction of souls. Amen.

Glory Be to the Father

Glory be to the Father, and to the Son, and to the Holy Spirit. As it was in the beginning, is now, and ever shall be, world without end. Amen.

Novenas

NOVENA TO THE SACRED HEART

O Divine Jesus who has said, "Ask and you shall receive; seek and you shall find; knock and it shall be opened unto you," behold me prostrate at Thy feet. Animated with a lively faith and confidence in the promises dictated by Thy Sacred Heart and pronounced by Thy adorable lips, I come to ask Thy aid (*here mention your request*).

From whom shall I ask, O Sweet Jesus, if not from Thee whose heart is an inexhaustible source of all graces and merits? Where shall I seek if not in the treasure which contains all the riches of Thy clemency and bounty? Where shall I knock if it be not at the door of Thy Sacred Heart through which God Himself comes to us and through which we go to God?

To Thee then, O Heart of Jesus, I have recourse. In Thee I find consolation when afflicted, protection when persecuted, strength when overwhelmed with trials and light in doubt and darkness. I firmly believe Thou canst bestow upon me the grace I implore even though it should require a miracle. Thou hast only to will it and my prayer is granted. I own I am most unworthy of Thy favors, O Jesus, but this is not a reason for

11

me to be discouraged. Thou art the God of mercies and Thou wilt not refuse a contrite and humble heart. Cast upon me a look of pity, I conjure Thee and Thy compassionate Heart will find in my miseries and weakness a pressing motive for granting my petition.

But, O Sacred Heart, whatever may be Thy decision with regard to my request I will never cease to adore, love, praise and serve Thee. Deign, my Jesus, to accept this my act of perfect submission to the decrees of Thy adorable Heart which I sincerely desire may be fulfilled in and by me and all Thy creatures forever and ever.   Amen.

Act of Consecration to the Sacred Heart of Jesus

Most Sweet Jesus, redeemer of the human race, look down upon us humbly prostrate before Thy altar. We are Thine and Thine we wish to be, but to be more surely united with Thee, behold, each one of us freely consecrates himself today to Thy most Sacred Heart. Many indeed have never known Thee; many too, despising Thy precepts, have rejected Thee. Have mercy on them all, most merciful Jesus, and draw them to Thy Sacred Heart.

Be Thou King, O Lord, not only of the faithful who have never forsaken Thee but also of the prodigal children who have abandoned Thee. Grant that they may quickly return to their

Father's house lest they die of wretchedness and hunger.

Be Thou King of those who are deceived by erroneous opinions or whom discord keeps aloof and call them back to the harbor of truth and unity of faith so that soon there may be but one flock and one Shepherd.

Grant, O Lord, to Thy Church assurance of freedom and immunity from harm. Give peace and order to all nations and make the earth resound from pole to pole with one cry: Praise to the Divine Heart that wrought our salvation; to It be glory and honor forever.   Amen.

Special Prayer for Each Day

FIRST DAY

My God and my Lord, Jesus Christ, in deepest humility I kneel before Thee and adore Thy Divine Heart. No one dares to doubt that Thou wilt grant all graces necessary to our salvation. Didst Thou not say: "God alone is good" and art not Thou my very God? Is not Thy Heart the Heart of God who is all love?

Therefore, there can be no power that is able to hinder Thee from granting all our requests. Nothing is difficult for Thy omnipotence and Thy riches are infinite and can never be exhausted.

No matter how often I may have sinned against

Thee, I shall not despair because I know that Thou art God infinite in generosity and mercy, always ready to pardon every contrite and humble sinner.

O compassionate Heart of Jesus, God of solace, grant me comfort. Pardon me, come to my assistance. Say but the word and I shall find relief in my sore trials.

I place my hope in Thee. Let me not be confounded. O Heart of my omnipotent God, have mercy on me.

SECOND DAY

With the greatest confidence, I come to Thee, the fatherly Heart of Jesus, for I know that no father, were he ever so loving and solicitous, can possibly love his children as Thou hast always loved me. To whom, therefore, shall I go if not to Thee, the best of fathers and the author of all good? It is indeed true that I have grievously offended Thee, that I have neglected to honor Thee properly and have been guilty of ingratitude and so do not deserve to be numbered among Thy children. But although I forgot my duty to Thee as Thy child I know that Thou art still my beloved Father in heaven. Now, I, with a contrite heart, cast myself at Thy feet weeping over my sins and promising Thee that in the future I shall rather die than offend Thee again. I hope, in spite

14

of my sinfulness, to be received by Thee who hast so often sought me and then to taste Thy sweet forbearance toward me. O sweetest Heart of Jesus, help me with Thy grace so that I may carry out my resolution. Then, O Jesus, if my wishes are not contrary to Thy most holy Will, I beg of Thee (*mention favor*) for which I pray with confidence and which I hope to receive from Thy infinite goodness.

THIRD DAY

O beloved Jesus, my heart is deeply moved at the thought that Thou, Almighty God, should take upon Thyself our human nature in order to enable Thee to become our brother and to make us children of God. But Thy loving Heart was not satisfied to raise us to such high dignity. Thou didst also desire to make us partakers in Thy inheritance in the Kingdom of Heaven. How greatly are we not indebted to Thee for these favors. Oh how I grieve to think that until this very day I have been so ungrateful for Thy many gifts. Most humbly do I ask Thy forgiveness and pray that Thou mayest through the merits of Thy Sacred Heart grant me the grace to follow Thee in all things so that at my death Thy heavenly Father may find me worthy to be Thy brother in heaven. Furthermore, I beg of Thy most merciful Heart to have pity on me in my present need and grant me the favor which I hope to obtain from Thee.

FOURTH DAY

O sweetest Heart of Jesus, to whom shall I turn in all my sorrows if not to Thee, the faithful friend of our souls? Thou hast given Thy very life for me. How, then, canst Thou refuse me Thy assistance during my life? It is true, indeed, and I must confess this to Thee, that instead of relying on Thee only I have too often trusted to the love and friendship of creatures although I had frequently experienced their treachery. If I have thus insulted Thee in the past I promise in the future never to repeat the offense. I promise that henceforth in all my doubts, afflictions and needs I will have recourse to Thee only to find light, help, comfort and grace. Henceforth Thou alone shalt be my friend, upon Thee alone will I rely. Thy friendship shall be above all others. In fact, I promise to renounce all other friendships if they are an occasion of disloyalty to Thee. To manifest my perfect trust in Thee I will now beg of Thee to help me in my present need.

I pray Thee to be my "strong defense." Be to me a "medicine for immortality." By kindly granting this request, Thou wilt unite my heart more closely with Thine and make me forever grateful to Thy love. Do not permit my trust in

Thee to be confounded, Thou eternally faithful, benevolent and sweet Heart of Jesus.

FIFTH DAY

O Divine Saviour, the infinite love of Thy Sacred Heart was so inflamed for us that it brought Thee as a sacrifice of propitiation for our sins to the altar of the cross. Still, Thy love was not satisfied with this but permitted Thy Heart to be opened with a lance that through this wound we might behold the innermost love of this Heart and better understand Thy indescribable longing for our salvation. Thou hast given us the wounded Heart and Thou keepest it open for us not only that we may find therein a protection against the justice of the eternal Father whom we have offended by our sins but also that this source of grace and mercy may always be open to us in our needs. Why, then, do I come to Thee so seldom and so indifferently? Why do I not fly to this source of all grace? O dearest Jesus, may Thy Heart forgive me these insults which through want of confidence in Thee I have so often committed against Thee. Behold, I now come to Thee with living faith with the intention never to leave Thee. Here I shall seek what I need so much, first the forgiveness of my sins, the grace to do better, and Thy eternal love, and then I pray for Thy assistance in my present need.

SIXTH DAY

O Jesus, my divine model and teacher, what can I do when I see Thee, the Son of the Eternal Father, full of glory and honor, laden with the cross, walking the awful road to death, especially when thereby Thou showest me the way to salvation without selfishness but only for my benefit? O Jesus, what can I do but to have faith in Thee and requite Thy love by at least bearing my trials in patience and humility. And this particularly, my God, because I have so often experienced the great power which my passions have over me, and how seldom I can withstand the temptations of the world. How hard do I not find it to deny myself the pleasure to mortify my desires and to renounce the false splendor of the world although I know full well that all these things so easily lead me into sin. Oh give me strength to resist my passions and close my eyes to the allurements and charms of the world, help me to imitate Thy poverty, purity and humility, and send me trials with the strength to bear them humbly. Though I fear them, they are necessary for me. But I wish to follow Thee and become like to Thee. Therefore, permit me to drink also of Thy chalice of suffering. Heart of Jesus, burning for love of me, inflame my heart with love for Thee.

O my Divine Saviour, according to the clear words of Thy Holy Scriptures, Thou art in truth our advocate before Thy Father. Thou hast freely taken this office upon Thyself and dost unceasingly exercise it with faithful and loving zeal for all those who trust in Thee. Thy influence with the Father is so great that He cannot refuse Thee and that He always hears Thee as Thou hast testified at the grave of Lazarus. Filled with this faith and with confidence in Thy compassionate Heart, I come to Thee to plead my cause. I have offended Thy Father and have called the anger of His Majesty upon myself. I am heavily indebted to His strict justice and I have nothing wherewith to pay the debt and therefore must fear the punishment. Besides all this, I am in the present need . . . where only the power of the Father can help me. For the salvation of my soul I sorely need this grace. Oh may it come to me from the riches of Thy Father, O my beloved advocate, from Thy throne in heaven to Thy Father and to my Father, to Thy God and to my God, and reconcile me with Him. I repent sincerely of ever having offended Him. Repay my debts out of the infinite treasury of Thy merits and obtain for me assistance in my present trial and the grace which I need so much. In the "Our Father" Thou hast composed a prayer with which I will now approach the Father. Accompany me and with the entire fervor and power of Thy most Sacred Heart as my mediator, say with me: Our Father, who art in heaven. . . .

EIGHTH DAY

My God and my Saviour, Jesus Christ! I believe it to be an undeniable truth. I believe it firmly, O Jesus. Thou art my good shepherd. Even if Thou hadst not said it, I would nevertheless believe it because I know that Thou hast in my behalf always manifested the heart of a good shepherd. Would that I, during my entire life, had permitted the goodness and solicitude of Thy Heart to lead me; would that I had never departed from Thy side, for then I would never have suffered so much misery and tribulation. But alas, I was untrue to Thee so often that in consequence I fell into the abyss of sin and was mortally wounded. Now, however, Thy straying lamb calls to Thee from the depths of its misery. O my good Shepherd, have mercy on me; give me proof again of Thy compassionate Heart. After all that Thou hast thus far done for me I cannot believe that Thy Heart will reject me. Consequently, I beseech this Heart, I embrace it with confidence, and conjure Thee by all Thy merits that Thou obtain for me from Thy heavenly Father the forgiveness of my sins and the grace for a complete conversion. And then I also pray for the grace . . . of which I am so much in need and which I hope to receive as the fruit of this novena. O Heart of the good Shepherd, have mercy on me.

NINTH DAY

O adorable Saviour, Jesus Christ, I believe what Thy Holy Word teaches. I believe that Thou wast made a priest forever by the solemn oath of Thy eternal Father and that Thou offerest sacrifices forever. I believe that Thou offerest the most sublime, holy and pure sacrifice most pleasing to God in the fire of Thy love, Thy Heart, Thy infinite merits, even Thy entire self. Lastly, I believe that the profoundest compassion of Thy priestly Heart impels Thee to carry on the function of Thy priesthood forever and ever in order to reconcile Thy Father with us and to offer Him adoration, praise and thanksgiving for us as well as to entreat Him and grant us every needed grace.

Inspired by this faith I come to Thee, O loving Jesus. I place all my needs with great confidence into Thy priestly Heart and upon the altar of Thy Heart. The eternal Father cannot refuse anything to such a priest and his sacrifice. Remember me then in all the Masses in which Thou offerest Thyself today throughout the world. Let Thy petition ascend from Thy Sacred Heart that the eternal Father may deign, through

Thy merits, to forgive me all my sins which I detest from the bottom of my heart and in His Fatherly love to grant me the grace for which I have so ardently pleaded during this novena. O Sacred Heart, if the heavenly Father grant this request for Thy sake it will redound to Thy own glory because it will be a testimony to Thy Father's love for Thee. Procure this honor for Thyself and from the sanctuary of heaven bring me this desired grace so that my faith in Thee may be strengthened and that my love of Thee may be more and more enkindled, O Thou loving and priestly Heart of Jesus.

Litany of the Sacred Heart

Lord, have mercy on us.
Christ, have mercy on us.
Lord, have mercy on us.
Christ, hear us.
Christ, graciously hear us.
God, the Father of Heaven,*
God, the Son, Redeemer of the world,
God, the Holy Spirit,
Holy Trinity, one God,
Heart of Jesus, Son of the Eternal Father,
Heart of Jesus, formed by the Holy Spirit in the womb of the Virgin Mother,
Heart of Jesus, substanti-ally united to the Word of God,
Heart of Jesus, of Infinite Majesty,
Heart of Jesus, Sacred Temple of God,
Heart of Jesus, Tabernacle of the Most High,
Heart of Jesus, House of God and Gate of Heaven,
Heart of Jesus, burning furnace of charity,
Heart of Jesus, abode of Justice and Love,
Heart of Jesus, full of Goodness and Love,

* *Have mercy on us.*

22

Heart of Jesus, abyss of all virtues,*

Heart of Jesus, most worthy of all praise,

Heart of Jesus, King and Center of all hearts,

Heart of Jesus, in whom are all the treasures of wisdom and knowledge,

Heart of Jesus, in whom dwells the fullness of divinity,

Heart of Jesus, in whom the Father was well pleased,

Heart of Jesus, of whose fullness we have all received.

Heart of Jesus, desire of the everlasting hills,

Heart of Jesus, patient and most merciful,

Heart of Jesus, enriching all who invoke Thee,

Heart of Jesus, fountain of life and holiness,

Heart of Jesus, propitiation of our sins,

Heart of Jesus, loaded down with opprobrium,

Heart of Jesus, bruised for our offenses,

Heart of Jesus, obedient unto death,

Heart of Jesus, pierced with a lance,

Heart of Jesus, source of all consolation,

Heart of Jesus, our life and resurrection,

Heart of Jesus, our peace and reconciliation,

Heart of Jesus, victim of sin,

Heart of Jesus, salvation of those who trust in Thee,

Heart of Jesus, hope of those who die in Thee.

Heart of Jesus, delight of all the saints,

Lamb of God, who takes away the sins of the world, *spare us, O Lord.*

Lamb of God, who takes away the sins of the world, *graciously hear us, O Lord.*

Lamb of God, who takes away the sins of the world, *have mercy on us.*

Jesus meek and humble of heart,

Make our hearts like unto Thine.

* *Have mercy on us.*

Let Us Pray

O Almighty and Eternal God, look upon the Heart of Thy dearly beloved Son and upon the praise and satisfaction He offers Thee in behalf of sinners, and, being appeased, grant pardon to those who seek Thy mercy in the name of the same Jesus Christ, Thy Son,

23

who lives and reigns with Thee in the unity of the Holy Spirit, world without end. Amen.

General Prayers

Morning Offering

O Jesus, through the immaculate heart of Mary, I offer Thee my prayers, works and sufferings of this day, for all the intentions of Thy Sacred Heart, in union with the Holy Sacrifice of the Mass throughout the world, in reparation for my sins, and for the general intention recommended this month.

Act of Reparation

O Heart of Jesus, whose overflowing charity for men is requited by so much forgetfulness, negligence and contempt, behold us prostrate before Thy altar, eager to repair by a special act of homage the cruel indifference and injuries to which Thy loving Heart is everywhere subject.

Mindful, alas, that we ourselves have had a share in such great indignities, which we now deplore from the depths of our hearts, we humbly ask Thy pardon and declare our readiness to atone by voluntary expiation not only for our own personal offenses; but also for the sins of those who, straying far from the path of salvation, refuse in their obstinate infidelity to follow Thee, their Shepherd and Leader, or, renouncing the vows of their Baptism, have cast off the sweet yoke of Thy law.

We are now resolved to expiate each and every deplorable outrage committed against Thee; we are determined to make amends for the manifold offenses against Christian modesty in unbecoming dress and behavior, for all the foul seductions laid to ensnare the feet of the innocent, for the frequent violation of Sundays and holydays, and the shocking blasphemies uttered against Thee and Thy Saints. We wish also to make amends for the insults to which Thy Vicar on earth and Thy priests are subjected, for the profanation by conscious neglect or terrible acts of sacrilege, of the very Sacrament of Thy Divine love; and lastly for the public crimes of nations, who resist the rights and teaching authority of the Church which Thou hast founded.

Would, O Divine Jesus, we were able to wash away such abominations with our blood. We now offer, in reparation for these violations of Thy Divine honor, the satisfaction Thou didst once make to Thy eternal Father on the Cross and which Thou dost continue to renew daily on our altars; we offer it in union with the acts of atonement of Thy Virgin Mother and all the saints and of the pious faithful on earth; and we sincerely promise to make recompense, as far as we can with the help of Thy grace, for all neglect of Thy great love and for the sins we and others have committed in the past. Henceforth, we will live a life of unwavering faith, of purity of conduct, of perfect observance of the precepts of the Gospel and especially that of charity. We promise to the best of our power to prevent others from offending Thee and to bring as many as possible to follow Thee.

O loving Jesus, through the intercession of the Blessed Virgin Mary, our model in reparation, deign to receive the voluntary offering we make of this act of expiation; and by the crowning gift of perseverance keep us faithful unto death in our duty and the allegiance we owe to Thee, so that we may all one day come to that happy home, where Thou with the Father and the Holy Spirit livest and reignest, God, world without end. Amen.

Petition to the Sacred Heart

O Sacred Heart of Jesus, I have asked You for many favors but I plead for this one (*here mention request*). Take it, place it in Your open, broken Heart, and when the Eternal Father sees it covered with the mantle of Your most Precious Blood, He will not refuse it. It is not my prayer, but Yours. O Sacred Heart of Jesus, I place all my trust in Thee.

For the Souls in Purgatory

O Divine Heart of Jesus, grant, we beseech Thee, eternal rest to the souls in purgatory, the final grace to those who shall die today, true repentance to sinners, the light of faith to pagans and Thy blessing to me and mine.

NOVENA TO THE HOLY SPIRIT

Hymn

Come, Holy Ghost

Come, Holy Ghost, Creator blest!
And in our souls take up Thy rest;
Come with Thy grace and heavenly aid
To fill the hearts which Thou hast made;
To fill the hearts which Thou hast made.

O Comforter! to Thee we cry,
Thou heavenly gift of God most High;
Thou fount of life and fire of love,
And sweet anointing from above;
And sweet anointing from above.

Novena Prayer

O Holy Spirit, divine Consoler! I adore you as my true God. I bless you by uniting myself to the praises you receive from the angels and the saints. I offer you my whole heart, and I render you heartfelt thanks for all the benefits that you have bestowed and do unceasingly bestow upon the world. You who are the author of all super-natural gifts and who did enrich with immense favors the soul of the Blessed Virgin Mary, the Mother of God, I beseech you to visit me by your grace and your love, and grant me the favor I so earnestly seek in this novena . . . O Holy Spirit, spirit of truth, come into our hearts: shed the brightness of your light on all nations, that they may be one in faith and pleasing to you.   Amen.

Come, O Holy Spirit, fill the hearts of Thy faithful, and kindle in them the fire of Thy love.

FIRST DAY

O Holy Spirit, bestow upon us your seven holy gifts. Enlighten our understanding that we may know you. Give us wisdom that your will may be clear to us and that we may accept it. Grant us the gift of counsel that we may always perceive what is right. Fortify us that we may always be capable of fulfilling your divine will. Inspire us with the spirit of learning that we may be able to penetrate more deeply into the truths which you have revealed. Let our hearts be steeped in the spirit of childlikeness that we may bring you joy. Let us have a proper fear of God that we may never grieve you or wander from the path of goodness. Give us the fullness of your gifts that we may glorify you.   Amen.

Look with compassion upon us, O Holy

Spirit, and grant us the favor we seek in this novena . . . if it be in accordance with your holy will.

SECOND DAY

O Holy Spirit, make me faithful in every thought, and grant that I may always listen to your voice, and watch for your light, and follow your gracious inspirations. I cling to you, and give myself to you, and ask you by your compassion to watch over me in my weakness. Holding the pierced feet of Jesus, looking at his five wounds, trusting in his precious blood, adoring his opened side and stricken heart, I implore you, adorable Spirit, helper of my infirmity, to keep me in your grace, now and always.   Amen.

Come, O Holy Spirit, fill the hearts of Thy faithful, and kindle in them the fire of Thy love.

THIRD DAY

Heavenly Father, you have called me to be a member of the mystical body of your Son, Jesus Christ, and to be a temple of the Holy Spirit. I ask you to give me the seven gifts of the Holy Spirit: wisdom, that I may understand the follies of this world; understanding, that I may grasp more fully the meaning of my existence and the purpose of all things in the world; counsel, that I may always choose the proper way; fortitude, that I may remain faithful to you under the pressure of temptation; piety, that I may revere you in all I do, think, or say; fear of the Lord, that should the motive of love fail me, I may be quickly awakened to the eternal consequences of my deeds.

Come, O Holy Spirit, fill the hearts of Thy faithful, and kindle in them the fire of Thy love.

FOURTH DAY

O God, who today by the light of the Holy Spirit did instruct the hearts of the faithful, give us, by the light of the same Holy Spirit, a love for what is right and just and a constant enjoyment of His comforts. Pray, O Holy Spirit, that I may strive to learn more of my faith; that I may ever be conscious that reason in all its human magnificence is capable of grasping but a glimpse of the reality that is God. Pray that I may accept as the motto of my life: "All for the greater glory of God."

Come, O Holy Spirit, fill the hearts of Thy faithful, and kindle in them the fire of Thy love.

FIFTH DAY

Come, O Spirit of sanctity, from the glory of heaven and send forth the radiance of your

31

light. Father of all the poor, light and peace of all hearts, come with your countless gifts. Consoler in desolation; refreshment full of loveliness, come, dear friend of my soul. In weariness send repose; breathe gently the cool refreshing breeze; console the desolate who weep alone. O Light of beatitude, make our hearts ready; come enter into our souls. Without your grace, man stands alone; he cannot be good or sure. Cleanse what is soiled; heal what is wounded; moisten what is arid. Bend the stubborn will; warm the cold heart; guide the wandering footstep. O Holy Spirit, we beg you to give us grace through your sevenfold power. Give us merit for the present, and one day beatitude when we have finished our earthly journey. Amen.

Come, O Holy Spirit, fill the hearts of Thy faithful, and kindle in them the fire of Thy love.

SIXTH DAY

O Father in heaven, I beg you to send the Holy Spirit. May your Holy Spirit remind me when I am apt to forget your law, your love, your promises. May your Holy Spirit strengthen my memory to recall frequently your sanctity, omniscience, wisdom and goodness, faithfulness and love. May your Holy Spirit encourage me when I am slothful; strengthen me when I am weak; enlighten me when I no longer can help myself. Breathe into me, O Holy Spirit, that my mind may turn to what is holy. Move me, that I may do what is holy. Stir me, that I may love what is holy. Strengthen me, that I may preserve what is holy. Protect me, Holy Spirit, that I may never lose what is holy.

Come, O Holy Spirit, fill the hearts of Thy faithful, and kindle in them the fire of Thy love.

SEVENTH DAY

Come, Holy Spirit, creator of all things: come, visit our hearts with your power. Fill with grace, friendly guest, the hearts which you have created. You are called the Consoler, gift from the hand of God, source of life, light, love, and flame, highest good. You are the pledge of sevenfold grace, finger of the Father's hand, promised us by Him, and you make our tongues speak the truth. Cast light on our senses, pour love into our hearts. Grant our weak bodies strength that they may never grow weary of doing good. Keep the enemy far from us, give us peace always, let us willingly follow in your footsteps that we may be far removed from sin. Grant that through you we may grow in knowledge of the Father and of the Son, and that we may ever strongly believe in you, the Spirit of both. Praise and honor be forever to the Father on the highest throne, in the risen Son of God, in the Consoler.   Amen.

Come, O Holy Spirit, fill the hearts of Thy
faithful, and kindle in them the fire of Thy love.

EIGHTH DAY

O Holy Spirit, life and light of the Church,
give us thoughts higher than our own thoughts,
and prayers better than our own prayers, and
powers beyond our own powers, that we may
love and live, imitating Jesus Christ, our Lord
and Savior. Come to us, Holy Spirit, come, one
with the Father and the Son. Vouchsafe to dwell
within our souls and quickly make our hearts
your own. Quench you the fires of hate and
strife, the wasting fever of the heart. From perils
guard our feeble life and to our souls thy peace
impart. Let voice and mind and heart and
strength confess and glorify your name and let
the fire of charity burn bright and other hearts
inflame.   Amen.

Come, O Holy Spirit, fill the hearts of Thy
faithful, and kindle in them the fire of Thy love.

NINTH DAY

O Lord, Holy Spirit, grant me sight to see
the wondrous promise of divine love; insight to
see my own weakness; delight in your divine
presence in my soul which you have made your

temple through sanctifying grace. I pray, O Holy Spirit, that I be not doubting; that I be spared the pain of being alone without trust or hope in Christ; that my prayer may always be "My Lord and my God!" I pray that I may acquire a sense of retreat to prayer and recollection at various times in my daily life; for prayer is the bond that joins us to Christ. I pray that I may be aware of the physical needs of the poor and that I may share what I can with them in the charitable works of the Church. I pray, O Holy Spirit, that you will in your mercy grant me the favor I have sought in this novena. . . .

Come, O Holy Spirit, fill the hearts of Thy faithful, and kindle in them the fire of Thy love.

"He who asks of God in faith things needful for this life is sometimes mercifully heard and sometimes mercifully not heard. For the Physician knows better than the patient what will avail for the sick man."

Holy Spirit, Lord of Light,
From Thy throne in splendor bright
Shed on us a ray divine;
Come and from Thy boundless store
On our hearts Thy treasures pour;
Come and make us truly Thine.

O Thou blessed light divine,
Shine within these hearts of Thine,
And our inmost being fill!

Heal our wounds: our strength renew;
On our dryness pour Thy dew;
Wash our stains of guilt away;
Bend and sway our stubborn will;
From our hearts remove the chill;
Guide our footsteps when we stray.

NOVENA TO ST. JUDE

St. Jude, glorious apostle, faithful servant and friend of Jesus, the name of the traitor has caused you to be forgotten by many. But the Church honors and invokes you universally as the patron of hopeless cases, and of things despaired of. Pray for me who am so distressed. Make use, I implore you, of that particular privilege accorded you to bring visible and speedy help where help was almost despaired of. Come to my assistance in this great need that I may receive the consolation and succor of heaven in all my necessities, tribulations and sufferings particularly . . . (*here make your request*) and that I may bless God with you and all the elect throughout eternity. St. Jude, apostle, martyr and relative of our Lord Jesus Christ, of Mary and of Joseph, intercede for us!

Special Prayers for Each Day

FIRST DAY

O blessed apostle St. Jude, who labored so zealously among the Gentiles in many lands, and performed numerous miracles in needy and despairing cases, we invoke you to take a special interest in us and our needs. We feel that you understand us in a particular way. Hear our prayers and our petitions and plead for us in all our necessities especially . . . May we be patient in learning God's holy will and courageous in carrying it out.

St. Jude, pray for us!
My Jesus, mercy!

SECOND DAY

O blessed apostle Jude, who has been instrumental in gathering us here together this day, grant us that we may always serve Jesus Christ as He deserves to be served, giving of our best efforts in living as He wishes us to live. May we so dispose our hearts and minds that God will always be inclined to listen to our prayers and petitions, especially those petitions which we entrust to your care and for which we ask you to plead for us. . . .

Grant that we may be enlightened as to what is best for us, in the present and future, not forgetting the blessings we have received in the past.

St. Jude, pray for us!
My Jesus, mercy!

THIRD DAY

O St. Jude, apostle of Jesus Christ, you who have so faithfully and devotedly helped to spread His Gospel of Light, we who are gathered together today in your honor, ask and petition you to remember us and our needs. Especially do we pray for . . . May it also please our Lord to lend an ear to your supplications in our behalf. Grant that we may ever pray with fervor and devotion, resigning ourselves humbly to the divine will, seeing God's purpose in all our trials and knowing that He will leave no sincere prayer unanswered in some way.

St. Jude, pray for us!

My Jesus, mercy!

FOURTH DAY

St. Jude, you were called to be one of Christ's chosen apostles and labored to bring men to a knowledge and love of God; listen with compassion to those gathered together to honor you and ask your intercession. In this troubled world of ours we have many trials, difficulties and temptations. Plead for us in the heavenly court, asking that our petitions may be answered, especially the particular one we have in mind at this moment . . . May it please God to answer our prayers in the way that He knows best, giving us grace to see His purpose in all things.

St. Jude, pray for us!
My Jesus, mercy!

FIFTH DAY

O holy St. Jude, apostle and companion of Jesus Christ, you have shown us by example how to lead a life of zeal and devotion. We humbly entreat you today to hear our prayers and petitions. Especially do we ask you to obtain for us the following favor . . . Grant that in praying for present and future favors we may not forget the innumerable ones granted in the past but often return to give thanks. Humbly we resign ourselves to God's holy will, knowing that He alone knows what is best for us especially in our present needs and necessities.

St. Jude, pray for us!
My Jesus, mercy!

SIXTH DAY

St. Jude, apostle of Christ and helper in despairing cases, hear the prayers and petitions of those who are gathered together in your honor. In all our needs and desires may we only seek what is pleasing to God and what is best for our salvation. These, our petitions . . . we submit to you, asking you to obtain them for us, if they are for the good of our souls. We are resigned to

God's holy will in all things, knowing that He will leave no sincere prayer unanswered in some way though it may be in a way unexpected by us.

St. Jude, pray for us!

My Jesus, mercy!

SEVENTH DAY

O holy apostle St. Jude, in whose honor we are gathered today, may we never forget that our Lord and Savior Jesus Christ chose you to be one of His twelve apostles. Because of this and of the martyrdom you suffered for the Faith, we know you are a close friend of Almighty God. Therefore we do not hesitate to petition you in our necessities, especially . . . We humbly submit ourselves to the will of God, knowing full well that no sincere prayer is ever left unanswered. May we see God's good and gracious purpose working in all our trials.

St. Jude, pray for us!

My Jesus, mercy!

EIGHTH DAY

O St. Jude, apostle of Christ, pray that we may ever imitate the Divine Master and live according to His will. May we cooperate with the grace of God and ever remain pleasing in His

sight. Especially do we ask you to plead for us
and obtain whatsoever is necessary for our salvation. Forget not our special petitions . . . May
we always be thankful to God for the blessings
we have received in the past. Whatsoever we
ask for the present or future, we submit to the
divine will, realizing that God knows best what
is good for us. We know He will respond to our
prayers and petitions in one way or another.

St. Jude, pray for us!

My Jesus, mercy!

NINTH DAY

O holy St. Jude, apostle and martyr, grant
that we may so dispose our lives that we may
always be pleasing to God. In working out our
salvation in this life we have many needs and
necessities. Today we turn to you, asking you to
intercede for us and obtain for us the favors we
ask of God. Especially do we petition for . . .

May we not so much seek temporal good but
rather what will avail our souls, knowing that
it will profit us nothing if we gain the whole
world yet suffer the loss of our soul.

Therefore, may we incline ourselves toward
the divine will, seeing God's good and gracious
purpose in all our trials.

St. Jude, pray for us!

My Jesus, mercy!

Litany to St. Jude

(*For private use only*)

Lord, have mercy on us.
Christ, have mercy on us.
Lord, have mercy on us.
Christ, hear us.
Christ, graciously hear us.
God the Father of heaven, *have mercy on us.*
God the Son, Redeemer of the world, *have mercy on us.*
God the Holy Spirit, *have mercy on us.*
Holy Trinity, one God, *have mercy on us.*

St. Jude, relative of Jesus and Mary,*
St. Jude, while on earth deemed worthy to see Jesus and Mary, and to enjoy their company,
St. Jude, raised to the dignity of an apostle,
St. Jude, who had the honor of beholding your Divine Master humble Himself to wash your feet,
St. Jude, who at the Last Supper did receive the Holy Eucharist from the hands of Jesus,
St. Jude, who after the profound grief which the death of your beloved Master caused you, had the consolation of beholding Him risen from the dead, and of assisting at His glorious ascension,
St. Jude, who was filled with the Holy Spirit on the day of Pentecost,
St. Jude, who did preach the Gospel in Persia,
St. Jude, who did convert many people to the Faith,
St. Jude, who did perform wonderful miracles in the power of the Holy Spirit,
St. Jude, who did restore an idolatrous king to health of both soul and body,
St. Jude, who did impose silence on demons, and confound their oracles,
St. Jude, who did foretell to a weak prince, an honorable peace with his powerful enemy,
St. Jude, who did take from deadly serpents the power of injuring man,
St. Jude, who, disregarding the threats of the im-

* *Pray for us.*

43

pious, did courageously preach the doctrine of Christ,*

St. Jude, who did gloriously suffer martyrdom for the love of thy Divine Master,

Blessed apostle, with confidence, we invoke you!

Blessed apostle, with confidence, we invoke you!

Blessed apostle, with confidence, we invoke you!

St. Jude, help of the hopeless, aid me in my distress!

St. Jude, help of the hopeless, aid me in my distress!

St. Jude, help of the hopeless, aid me in my distress!

That by your intercession both priests and people of the Church may obtain an ardent zeal for the Faith of Jesus Christ, *we beseech you, hear us!*

That you would defend our Sovereign Pontiff and obtain peace and unity for the Church, *we beseech you, hear us!*

That all unbelievers may be converted to the true Faith, *we beseech you, hear us!*

That faith, hope and charity may increase in our hearts, *we beseech you, hear us!*

That we may be delivered from all evil thoughts, and from all the snares of the devil, *we beseech you, hear us!*

That you would vouchsafe to aid and protect all those who honor you, *we beseech you, hear us!*

That you would preserve us from all sin and from all occasions of sin, *we beseech you, hear us!*

That you would defend us at the hour of death, against the fury of the devil and his evil spirits, *we beseech you, hear us!*

Lamb of God, who take away the sins of the world, *have mercy on us.*

Lamb of God, who take away the sins of the world, *have mercy on us.*

Lamb of God, who take away the sins of the world, *grant us peace.*

* Pray for us.

Let Us Pray

O Lord Jesus Christ, who has said, Ask and you shall

44

receive, seek and you shall find, knock and it shall be opened unto you, grant, we beseech you, to us who ask the gift of your most divine love, that with all our hearts, words and works, we may love You and never cease to praise You. Amen.

NOVENA TO
THE IMMACULATE CONCEPTION

Novena Prayer in Honor of
the Immaculate Conception

O Mary Immaculate, Lily of purity, I salute thee, because from the very first instant of thy conception thou wast filled with grace. I thank and adore the Most Holy Trinity for having imparted to thee favors so sublime. O, Mary, full of grace, help me to share, even though just a little, in the fullness of grace so wonderfully bestowed on thee in thy Immaculate Conception. With firm confidence in thy never-failing intercession, we beseech thee to obtain for us the intention of this novena . . . and also that purity of mind, heart and body necessary to unite us with God.   Amen.

O Mary, conceived without sin, pray for us who have recourse to thee.

O Mother of God, by thy Immaculate Conception, intercede for us with thy Divine Son, and obtain for us from Him, the favor for which we pray.

46

Special Prayer for Each Day

FIRST DAY

O most Holy Virgin, who wast pleasing to the Lord and became His Mother, immaculate in body and spirit, in faith and in love, look kindly on me as I implore thy powerful intercession. O most Holy Mother, who by thy blessed Immaculate Conception, from the first moment of thy conception did crush the head of the enemy, receive our prayers as we implore thee to present at the throne of God the favor we now request. . . .

O Mary of the Immaculate Conception, Mother of Christ, you had influence with your Divine Son while upon earth; you have the same influence now in heaven. Pray for us and obtain for us from Him the granting of my petition if it be the Divine Will.   Amen.

SECOND DAY

O Mary, ever blessed Virgin, Mother of God, Queen of angels and of saints, I salute you with the most profound veneration and filial devotion as I contemplate your holy Immaculate Conception. I thank you for your maternal protection and for the many blessings that I have received through your wondrous mercy and most powerful intercession. In all my necessities I have recourse to you with unbounded confidence. O

47

Mother of Mercy, I beseech you now to hear my prayer and to obtain for me of your Divine Son the favor that I so earnestly request in this novena . . .

O Mary of the Immaculate Conception, Mother of Christ, you had influence with your Divine Son while upon earth; you have the same influence now in heaven. Pray for us and obtain for us from Him the granting of my petition if it be the Divine Will. Amen.

THIRD DAY

O Blessed Virgin Mary, glory of the Christian people, joy of the universal Church and Mother of Our Lord, speak thou for us to the Heart of Jesus, who is Thy Son and our brother. O Mary, who by thy holy Immaculate Conception did enter the world free from stain, do thou in thy mercy obtain for me from Jesus the special favor which I now so earnestly seek . . .

O Mary of the Immaculate Conception, Mother of Christ, you had influence with your Divine Son while upon earth; you have the same influence now in heaven. Pray for us and obtain for us from Him the granting of my petition if it be the Divine Will. Amen.

FOURTH DAY

O Mary, Mother of God, endowed in your glorious Immaculate Conception with the full-

48

ness of grace; unique among women in that you are both mother and virgin: mother of Christ and virgin of Christ, we ask thee to look down with a tender heart from thy throne and listen to our prayers as we earnestly ask that you obtain for us the favor for which we now plead . . .

O Mary of the Immaculate Conception, Mother of Christ, you had influence with your Divine Son while upon earth; you have the same influence now in heaven. Pray for us and obtain for us from Him the granting of my petition if it be the Divine Will.   Amen.

FIFTH DAY

O God, who, by the Immaculate Conception of the Virgin Mary, didst prepare a fitting dwelling for Thy Son, we beseech Thee that as by the foreseen death of the same, Thy Son, Thou didst preserve her from all stain of sin, so grant that, through her intercession, we may be favored with the granting of the grace which we seek for at this time . . .

O Mary of the Immaculate Conception, Mother of Christ, you had influence with your Divine Son while upon earth; you have the same influence now in heaven. Pray for us and obtain for us from Him the granting of my petition if it be the Divine Will.   Amen.

SIXTH DAY

Glorious and immortal Queen of Heaven, we profess our firm belief in thy Immaculate Conception pre-ordained for thee in the merits of Thy Divine Son. We rejoice with thee in thy Immaculate Conception. To the One and ever-reigning God, Father, Son and Holy Spirit, Three in one Person, one in nature, we offer thanks for thy blessed Immaculate Conception. O Mother of the Word made Flesh, listen to our petition as we ask this special grace during this novena . . .

O Mary of the Immaculate Conception, Mother of Christ, you had influence with your Divine Son while upon earth; you have the same influence now in heaven. Pray for us and obtain for us from Him the granting of my petition if it be the Divine Will. Amen.

SEVENTH DAY

O Immaculate Virgin, Mother of God and my mother, from the sublime heights of thy dignity turn thy merciful eyes upon me while I, full of confidence in thy bounty and keeping in mind thy Immaculate Conception and fully conscious of thy power, beg of thee to come to my aid and ask thy Divine Son to grant the favor I earnestly seek in this novena . . . if it be beneficial for my immortal soul and the souls for whom I pray.

O Mary of the Immaculate Conception, Mother of Christ, you had influence with your Divine Son while upon earth; you have the same influence now in heaven. Pray for us and obtain for us from Him the granting of my petition if it be the Divine Will.   Amen.

EIGHTH DAY

O most gracious Virgin Mary, beloved Mother of Jesus Christ, my Redeemer, intercede with Him for me that I be granted the favor which I petition for so earnestly in this novena . . . O Mother of the Word Incarnate, we feel animated with confidence that your prayers in our behalf will be graciously heard before the throne of God. O glorious Mother of God, in memory of your joyous Immaculate Conception, hear our prayers and obtain for us our petitions.

O Mary of the Immaculate Conception, Mother of Christ, you had influence with your Divine Son while upon earth; you have the same influence now in heaven. Pray for us and obtain for us from Him the granting of my petition if it be the Divine Will.   Amen.

NINTH DAY

O Mother of the King of the Universe, most

perfect member of the human race, "our tainted nature's solitary boast," we turn to you as mother, advocate and mediatrix. O Holy Mary, assist me in my present necessity. By thy Immaculate Conception, O Mary conceived without sin, I humbly beseech thee from the bottom of my heart to intercede for me with thy Divine Son and ask that I be granted the favor for which I now plead . . .

O Mary of the Immaculate Conception, Mother of Christ, you had influence with your Divine Son while upon earth; you have the same influence now in heaven. Pray for us and obtain for us from Him the granting of my petition if it be the Divine Will.   Amen.

Litany of the Blessed Virgin

(Also called "The Litany of Loreto")

We fly to your patronage, O holy Mother of God, despise not our petitions in our necessities but deliver us from all dangers, O ever glorious and blessed Virgin.

Lord, have mercy on us.
Christ, have mercy on us.
Lord, have mercy on us.
Christ, hear us.
Christ, graciously hear us.
God the Father of Heaven, *have mercy on us.*
God the Son, Redeemer of the world, *have mercy on us.*

God the Holy Spirit, *have mercy on us.*
Holy Trinity, one God, *have mercy on us.*

Holy Mary,*
Holy Mother of God,
Holy Virgin of virgins,
Mother of Christ,
_____
* *Pray for us.*

Mother of divine grace,*
Mother most pure,
Mother most chaste,
Mother inviolate,
Mother undefiled,
Mother most amiable,
Mother most admirable,
Mother of Good Counsel,
Mother of our Creator,
Mother of our Redeemer,
Virgin most prudent,
Virgin most venerable,
Virgin most renowned,
Virgin most powerful,
Virgin most merciful,
Virgin most faithful,
Mirror of justice,
Seat of wisdom,
Cause of our joy,
Spiritual vessel,
Vessel of honor,
Singular vessel of devotion,
Mystical rose,
Tower of David,
Tower of ivory,
House of Gold,
Ark of the covenant,
Gate of heaven,
Morning star,
Health of the sick,
Refuge of sinners,
Comforter of the afflicted,
Help of Christians,

Queen of Angels,
Queen of Confessors,
Queen of Patriarchs,
Queen of Prophets,
Queen of Martyrs,
Queen of Apostles,
Queen of Virgins,
Queen of All Saints,
Queen conceived without original sin,
Queen assumed into heaven,
Queen of the most holy Rosary,
Queen of Peace,

Lamb of God, who take away the sins of the world, *spare us, O Lord.*
Lamb of God, who take away the sins of the world, *graciously hear us, O Lord.*
Lamb of God, who take away the sins of the world, *have mercy on us.*
Pray for us, O holy Mother of God.
That we may be made worthy of the promises of Christ.

* *Pray for us.*

Let Us Pray

Pour forth, we beseech Thee, O Lord, Thy grace into our hearts; that as we have known the Incarnation of Christ Thy Son by the message of an angel, so, by His Passion and Cross, we may be brought to the glory

53

of His resurrection: through the same Christ Our Lord.
Amen.

Memorare

Remember, O most gracious Virgin Mary, that
never was it known that anyone who fled to thy
protection, implored thy help and sought thy
intercession was left unaided. Inspired with this
confidence, I fly unto thee, O Virgin of virgins,
my mother. To thee I come, before thee I stand
sinful and sorrowful. O Mother of the Word
Incarnate, despise not my petitions, but in thy
mercy hear and grant my prayer.   Amen.

NOVENA TO ST. JOSEPH

O Glorious St. Joseph, faithful follower of Jesus Christ, to you do we raise our hearts and hands to implore your powerful intercession in obtaining from the benign heart of Jesus all the helps and graces necessary for our spiritual and temporal welfare, particularly for the grace of a happy death and the special favor we now implore . . .

O Guardian of the Word Incarnate, we feel animated with confidence that your prayers in our behalf will be graciously heard before the throne of God.

O Glorious St. Joseph, through the love you bear to Jesus Christ and for the glory of His name, hear our prayers and obtain our petitions.

FIRST DAY

O great St. Joseph, with feelings of unlimited confidence, I beg thee to bless this novena that I begin in thy honor. "Thou are never invoked in vain" says the seraphic Theresa of Jesus. Be thou then to me what thou hast been to that

Spouse of the Sacred Heart of Jesus and graciously hear me as thou didst her. Amen.

SECOND DAY

O Blessed St. Joseph, tender-hearted father, faithful guardian of Jesus, chaste spouse of the Mother of God, I pray and beseech thee to offer to God the Father, His divine Son, bathed in blood on the Cross for sinners, and through the thrice holy name of Jesus obtain for us of the eternal Father the favor for which we implore your intercession . . .

Amid the splendors of eternity, forget not the sorrows of those who suffer, those who pray, those who weep; stay the almighty arm which smites us, that by thy prayers and those of thy most holy Spouse, the Heart of Jesus may be moved to pity and to pardon. Amen.

St. Joseph, pray for us.

THIRD DAY

Blessed St. Joseph, enkindle in my cold heart a spark of thy charity. May God be always the first and only object of my affections. Keep my soul always in sanctifying grace and, if I should be so unhappy as to lose it, give me the strength to recover it immediately by a sincere repentance. Help me to such a love of my God as will always keep me united to Him.

O Glorious St. Joseph, through the love you bear to Jesus Christ and for the glory of His name, hear our prayers and obtain our petitions.

FOURTH DAY

St. Joseph, pride of heaven, unfailing hope for our lives, and support of those on earth, graciously accept our prayer of praise. You were appointed spouse of the chaste Virgin by the Creator of the world. He willed that you be called "father" of the Word and serve as agent of our salvation. May the triune God who has bestowed upon you heavenly honors, be praised forever. And may He grant us through your merits the joy of a blessed life and a favorable answer to our petition . . .

St. Joseph, pray for us.

FIFTH DAY

O holy St. Joseph, what a lesson your life is for me, ever so eager to appear so anxious to display before the eyes of men the graces that I owe entirely to the liberality of God. In addition to the special favor for which I plead in this novena . . . obtain that I may attribute to God the glory of all things, that I may love the humble and hidden life, that I may not desire any other position than the one given me by Providence and that I may always be a docile instrument in the hands of God.

St. Joseph, pray for us.

SIXTH DAY

O Glorious St. Joseph, appointed by the Eternal Father as the guardian and protector of the life of Jesus Christ, the comfort and support of His Holy Mother, and the instrument in His great design for the Redemption of mankind; thou who had the happiness of living with Jesus and Mary, and of dying in their arms, be moved with the confidence we place in thee, and procure for us from the Almighty, the particular favor which we humbly ask through your intercession . . .

St. Joseph, pray for us.

SEVENTH DAY

O faithful and prudent St. Joseph, watch over my weakness and my inexperience; obtain for me that prudence which reminds me of my end, which directs my paths and which protects me from every danger. Pray for me, then, O great Saint, and by thy love for Jesus and Mary, and by their love for thee, obtain for me the favor I ask in this novena . . .

St. Joseph, pray for us.

EIGHTH DAY

O Blessed Joseph, to whom it was given not only to see and to hear that God whom many kings longed to see and saw not; to hear and heard not; but also to carry Him in thy arms, to embrace Him, to clothe Him, and to guard and defend Him, come to my assistance and intercede with Him to look favorably on my present petition . . .

St. Joseph, pray for us.

NINTH DAY

O good St. Joseph, help me to be like thee, gentle to those whose weakness leans on me; help me to give to those who seek my aid, succor that they may journey unafraid. Give me thy faith, that I may see the right shining above the victories of might. Give me thy hope that I may stand secure, untouched by doubting, steadfast to endure. Give me thy love that as the years increase an understanding heart may bring me peace. Give me thy purity that the hour of death finds me untouched by evil's breath. Give me thy love of labor that I shirk no lot in life that calls for honest work. Give me thy love of poverty so that I live contented, let wealth come or go. Give me thy courage that I may be strong; give me thy meekness to confess my wrong. Give me thy patience that I may possess the kingdom of my soul without distress. Help me, dear Saint, to live that when life ends I pass with thee to Jesus and His friends.

O Glorious St. Joseph, hear our prayers and obtain our petitions.

St. Joseph, pray for us.

Litany of St. Joseph

Lord, have mercy on us.
Christ, have mercy on us.
Lord, have mercy on us.
Christ, hear us.
Christ, graciously hear us.
God the Father of Heaven, *have mercy on us.*
God the Son, Redeemer of the world, *have mercy on us.*
God the Holy Spirit, *have mercy on us.*
Holy Trinity, one God, *have mercy on us.*
Holy Mary, *pray for us.*

St. Joseph,*
Renowned offspring of David,
Light of patriarchs,
Spouse of the Mother of God,
Chaste guardian of the Virgin,
Foster-father of the Son of God,
Diligent protector of Christ,
Head of the Holy Family,
Joseph most just,
Joseph most chaste,
Joseph most prudent,
Joseph most strong,
Joseph most obedient,
Joseph most faithful,
Mirror of patience,
Lover of poverty,
Model of laborers,
Glory of home life,
Guardian of virgins,
Pillar of families,
Solace of the wretched,
Hope of the sick,
Patron of the dying,
Terror of demons,
Protector of Holy Church,
Lamb of God, who take

_____
* *Pray for us.*

60

away the sins of the world, *spare us, O Lord.* Lamb of God, who take away the sins of the world, *graciously hear us, O Lord.* Lamb of God, who take away the sins of the world, *have mercy on us.*

He made him the lord of His household. *And prince over all His possessions.*

Let Us Pray

O God, who in Thy ineffable providence didst vouchsafe to choose blessed Joseph to be the spouse of Thy most holy Mother, grant, we beseech Thee, that we may have for our advocate in heaven him whom we venerate as our protector on earth, who lives and reigns world without end. Amen.

NOVENA TO OUR LADY OF LOURDES

Daily Novena Prayer
to Our Lady of Lourdes

Be blessed, O most pure Virgin, for having vouchsafed to manifest thyself shining with life, sweetness and beauty, in the Grotto of Lourdes, saying to the child, St. Bernadette: "I am the Immaculate Conception." A thousand times we congratulate thee upon thy Immaculate Conception. And now, O ever Immaculate Virgin, Mother of mercy, Health of the sick, Refuge of sinners, Comforter of the afflicted, you know my wants, my troubles, my sufferings; deign to cast upon me a look of mercy. By appearing in the Grotto of Lourdes, you were pleased to make it a privileged sanctuary, whence you dispense your favors, and already many have obtained the cure of their infirmities, both spiritual and corporal. I come, therefore, with the most unbounded confidence to implore your maternal intercession. Obtain for me, O loving Mother, the granting of my request . . . Through gratitude for your favors, I will endeavor to imitate your virtues, that I may one day share your glory.

Our Lady of Lourdes, Mother of Christ, you had influence with your Divine Son while upon earth. You have the same influence now in heaven. Pray for me; obtain for me from your Divine Son my special request if it be the Divine Will. Amen.

FIRST DAY

O Mary Immaculate, Our Lady of Lourdes, virgin and mother, queen of heaven, chosen from all eternity to be the Mother of the Eternal Word and in virtue of this title preserved from original sin, we kneel before thee as did little Bernadette at Lourdes and pray with childlike trust in thee that as we contemplate thy glorious appearance at Lourdes, you will look with mercy on our present petition and secure for us a favorable answer to the request for which we are making this novena . . .

O brilliant star of purity, Mary Immaculate, Our Lady of Lourdes, glorious in thy assumption, triumphant in thy coronation, show unto us the mercy of the Mother of God. Virgin Mary, queen and Mother, be our comfort, hope, strength and consolation. Amen.

Our Lady of Lourdes, pray for us.

St. Bernadette, pray for us.

SECOND DAY

Be blessed, O most pure Virgin, for having vouchsafed to manifest thyself shining with light, sweetness and beauty, in the Grotto of Lourdes, saying to the child, St. Bernadette: "I am the Immaculate Conception!" O Mary Immaculate, inflame our hearts with one ray of the burning love of thy pure heart. Let them be consumed with love for Jesus and for thee, in order that we may merit one day to enjoy thy glorious eternity. O dispenser of His graces here below, take into thy keeping and present to thy Divine Son the petition for which I am making this novena.

O brilliant star of purity, Mary Immaculate, Our Lady of Lourdes, glorious in thy assumption, triumphant in thy coronation, show unto us the mercy of the Mother of God. Virgin Mary, Queen and Mother, be our comfort, hope, strength and consolation. Amen.

Our Lady of Lourdes, pray for us.

St. Bernadette, pray for us.

THIRD DAY

"Thou art all fair, O Mary, and there is in thee no stain of original sin." O Mary, conceived without sin, pray for us who have recourse to thee. O brilliant star of sanctity, as on that lovely day, upon a rough rock in Lourdes you spoke to the child Bernadette and a fountain broke from the plain earth and miracles happened and the great shrine of Lourdes began, so now I beseech thee to hear my fervent prayer and do, I beseech thee, grant me the petition I now so earnestly seek . . .

O brilliant star of purity, Mary Immaculate, Our Lady of Lourdes, glorious in thy assumption, triumphant in thy coronation, show unto us the mercy of the Mother of God. Virgin Mary, Queen and Mother, be our comfort, hope, strength and consolation.   Amen.

Our Lady of Lourdes, pray for us.

St. Bernadette, pray for us.

FOURTH DAY

O Immaculate Queen of heaven, we thy wayward, erring children, join our unworthy prayers of praise and thanksgiving to those of the angels and saints and thine own that the One, Holy and Undivided Trinity may be glorified in heaven and on earth. Our Lady of Lourdes, as you looked down with love and mercy upon Bernadette as she prayed her rosary in the grotto, look down now, we beseech thee, with love and mercy upon us. From the abundance of graces granted thee by thy Divine Son, sweet Mother of God, give to each of us all that thy motherly heart sees we need and at this moment look with special favor on the grace we seek in this novena . . .

O brilliant star of purity, Mary Immaculate, Our Lady of Lourdes, glorious in thy assumption, triumphant in thy coronation, show unto us the mercy of the Mother of God. Virgin Mary, Queen and Mother, be our comfort, hope, strength and consolation.   Amen.

Our Lady of Lourdes, pray for us.

St. Bernadette, pray for us.

FIFTH DAY

O Mary Immaculate, Mother of God and our mother, from the heights of thy dignity look down mercifully upon us while we, full of confidence in thy unbounded goodness and confident that thy Divine Son will look favorably upon any request you make of Him in our behalf, we beseech thee to come to our aid and secure for us the favor we seek in this novena . . .

O brilliant star of purity, Mary Immaculate, Our Lady of Lourdes, glorious in thy assumption, triumphant in thy coronation, show unto us the mercy of the Mother of God. Virgin Mary, Queen and Mother, be our comfort, hope, strength and consolation.   Amen.

Our Lady of Lourdes, pray for us.

St. Bernadette, pray for us.

SIXTH DAY

O glorious Mother of God, so powerful under your special title of Our Lady of Lourdes, to you we raise our hearts and hands to implore your powerful intercession in obtaining from the benign Heart of Jesus all the helps and graces necessary for our spiritual and temporal welfare and for the special favor we so earnestly seek in this novena . . . O Lady of Bernadette, with the stars of heaven in your hair and the roses of earth at your feet, look with compassion upon us today as you did so long ago on Bernadette in the Grotto of Lourdes.

O brilliant star of purity, Mary Immaculate, Our Lady of Lourdes, glorious in thy assumption, triumphant in thy coronation, show unto us the mercy of the Mother of God. Virgin Mary, Queen and Mother, be our comfort, hope, strength and consolation.   Amen.

Our Lady of Lourdes, pray for us.

St. Bernadette, pray for us.

SEVENTH DAY

O Almighty God, who by the Immaculate Conception of the Blessed Virgin Mary did prepare a worthy dwelling place for Thy Son, we humbly beseech Thee that as we contemplate the apparition of Our Lady in the Grotto of Lourdes, we may be blessed with health of mind and body. And, O most gracious Mother Mary, beloved Mother of my Lord and Redeemer, look with favor upon us as you did that day on Bernadette and intercede with Him for us that the favor we now so earnestly seek may be granted to us . . .

O brilliant star of purity, Mary Immaculate, Our Lady of Lourdes, glorious in thy assumption, triumphant in thy coronation, show unto us the mercy of the Mother of God. Virgin Mary, Queen and Mother, be our comfort, hope, strength and consolation. Amen.

Our Lady of Lourdes, pray for us.

St. Bernadette, pray for us.

EIGHTH DAY

O Immaculate Mother of God, from heaven itself you came to appear to little Bernadette in the rough Grotto of Lourdes! And as Bernadette knelt at your feet and the magic spring burst forth and as multitudes have knelt ever since before your shrine, O Mother of God, I kneel before you today to ask that in your mercy you plead with your Divine Son to grant the special favor I seek in this novena . . .

O brilliant star of purity, Mary Immaculate, Our Lady of Lourdes, glorious in thy assumption, triumphant in thy coronation, show unto us the mercy of the Mother of God. Virgin Mary, Queen and Mother, be our comfort, hope, strength and consolation.   Amen.

Our Lady of Lourdes, pray for us.

St. Bernadette, pray for us.

NINTH DAY

O glorious Mother of God, to you do we raise our hearts and hands to implore your powerful intercession in obtaining from the benign heart of Jesus all the graces necessary for our spiritual and temporal welfare, particularly for the grace of a happy death. O Mother of our Divine Lord, as we conclude this novena for the special favor we seek at this time . . . we feel animated with confidence that your prayers in our behalf will be graciously heard. O Mother of my Lord, through the love you bear to Jesus Christ and for the glory of His Name, hear our prayers and obtain our petitions.

O brilliant star of purity, Mary Immaculate, Our Lady of Lourdes, glorious in thy assumption, triumphant in thy coronation, show unto us the mercy of the Mother of God. Virgin Mary, Queen and Mother, be our comfort, hope, strength and consolation.   Amen.

Our Lady of Lourdes, pray for us.

St. Bernadette, pray for us.

Litany of Our Lady of Lourdes

(*For private devotion only*)

Lord, have mercy on us.
Christ, have mercy on us.
Lord, have mercy on us.
Christ, hear us.
Christ, graciously hear us.
God the Father of Heaven, *have mercy on us.*
God the Son, redeemer of the world, *have mercy on us.*
God the Holy Spirit, *have mercy on us.*
Holy Trinity, one God, *have mercy on us.*

Exalted model of all mothers, Our Lady of Lourdes,*
Mother who did suffer so much,
Mother poor and without shelter,
Mother who did bear along forgotten roads the fruit of thy womb,
Who did find no other shelter for thy Son and thy God than a wild cave, and no other cradle than a manger,
Who did declare—"I am the Immaculate Conception,"
Who did appear to an humble peasant girl in order to teach us humility,
Who was clad in a white robe to remind us of purity,
Who did wear a girdle of blue to remind us of heaven,
Who did tread on a rose bush to remind us of the sufferings we must endure in order to merit heaven,
Who did carry the rosary to induce us to pray,
Who had thy hands joined and thy eyes raised to heaven to draw us to penance,
Who art the Star of Hope,
Who dost pray to the Sacred Heart of Jesus for us,
Who dost give strength to the clergy,
Who dost heal the sick,
Who art the health of the weak,
Refuge of sinners,
Comforter of the afflicted,

Our Lady of Lourdes, conceived without sin, *pray*
* *Pray for us.*

70

for us who have re-
course to thee.

Lamb of God, who take
away the sins of the
world, *spare us, O Lord*.

Lamb of God, who take
away the sins of the
world, *graciously hear
us, O Lord*.

Lamb of God, who take
away the sins of the
world, *have mercy on us*.

Pray for us, our Lady of
Lourdes, Holy Mother
of God.

*That we may be made
worthy of the promises
of Christ*.

Prayer

Our Lady of Lourdes, so fruitful in miracles, protect, with that hand which nothing can resist, our
Holy Father the Pope. Infuse into us the spirit of
faith, hope and charity. We all believe the truth of
thy apparitions, and the unlimited power with which
thy Divine Son has armed thee. Hence it is that we
have recourse to thee.

Hymn to Our Lady of Lourdes

Ave, Ave, Ave Maria!
Ave, Ave, Ave Maria!

Immaculate Mary!
Our hearts are on fire.
That title so wondrous
Fills all our desires!

We pray for God's glory,
May His Kingdom come;
We pray for His vicar,
Our Father, and Rome.

71

We pray for our Mother,
The Church upon earth;
And bless, sweetest Lady,
The land of our birth.

O Mary! O Mother!
Be Queen of our land;
May we be thy children
Guided by thy hand!

May we be thy children
And souls that now stray
From Jesus and Mary
In heresy's way.

For poor, sick, afflicted,
Thy mercy we crave;
And comfort the dying,
Thou light of the grave!

ROSARY NOVENA

The 54 day Rosary Novena consists of the daily recitation of five decades of the Rosary for twenty-seven days in petition and five decades for twenty-seven days in thanksgiving.

The Rosary is composed of fifteen decades, each decade consisting of one Our Father, ten Hail Marys, and one Glory Be to the Father, recited in honor of some mystery in the life of our Lord and of His Blessed Mother.

Prayer of Petition

(To be said for the first 27 days)

O Glorious Mother of God, Queen of the most holy Rosary, I beseech thee to accept this Rosary Novena which, as a crown of roses, I lay at thy feet. As I offer this prayer, most gracious Lady, I earnestly ask you to intercede for me with your Divine Son so that I may be granted the favor which I now seek through your powerful intercession . . .

Prayer of Thanksgiving

(To be said for the second 27 days)

O Glorious Mother of God, Queen of the most holy Rosary, I kneel in gratitude before thee to offer in thanksgiving this Rosary Novena which as a crown of roses I lay at thy feet. O most gracious Lady, I am truly grateful for your powerful intercession in behalf of the favor I so earnestly sought and have received. O Mother of God, keep me always under your special protection. Amen.

The Joyful Mysteries

First Mystery—The Annunciation

Meditation: Let us contemplate in this mystery how the angel Gabriel saluted our blessed Lady, "Full of Grace," and declared to her the Incarnation of our Lord Jesus Christ.

> *Say: One Our Father, Ten Hail Marys, One Glory Be to the Father.*

Prayer: O Holy Mary, Queen of virgins, by the most high mystery of the Incarnation of thy beloved Son, our Lord Jesus Christ, by which our salvation was so happily begun, obtain for us light to understand the benefit He has bestowed in vouchsafing to become our brother, and in giving us thee, His own most beloved Mother, to be our Mother also.   Amen.

I pray for the gift of the virtue of
Humility.

Second Mystery—The Visitation

Meditation: Let us contemplate in this mystery how the Blessed Virgin Mary, understanding from the angel that her cousin, St. Elizabeth, had conceived, went with haste into the mountains of Judea, to visit her, and remained with her three months.

Say: One Our Father, Ten Hail Marys, One Glory Be to the Father.

Prayer: O Holy Virgin, most spotless mirror of humility, by the exceeding charity which moved thee to visit thy holy cousin, St. Elizabeth, obtain that our hearts may be spiritually visited by thy most holy Son, and that, being purified from sin, we may praise and bless Him forever. Amen.

I pray for the gift of the virtue of
Charity.

Third Mystery—The Nativity

Meditation: Let us contemplate in this mystery how the Blessed Virgin Mary, when the time of her delivery was come, brought forth our Redeemer, Jesus Christ, at midnight, and laid him in a manger, because there was no room for Him in the inns at Bethlehem.

Say: One Our Father, Ten Hail Marys, One Glory Be to the Father.

Prayer: O most pure Mother of God, by thy exceeding happiness in being chosen to give birth to the Saviour of the world, I beseech thee to obtain for me grace to lead so pure and holy a life, that I may hereafter eternally sing the mercies of thy Son and His benefits to us, through thee.   Amen.

I pray for the gift of the virtue of
Poverty.

Fourth Mystery—The Presentation

Meditation: Let us contemplate in this mystery how the most Blessed Virgin Mary, on the day of her purification, presented the child Jesus in the Temple where holy Simeon, giving thanks to God, received Him with great devotion into his arms.

Say: One Our Father, Ten Hail Marys, One Glory Be to the Father.

Prayer: O Holy Virgin, most admirable mistress and pattern of obedience, who didst present in the Temple the Lord of the Temple, obtain that, with holy Simeon and devout Anna, we may praise and glorify Him forever.   Amen.

I pray for the gift of the virtue of Obedience.

Fifth Mystery—The Finding of the Child Jesus in the Temple

Meditation: Let us contemplate in this mystery how the Blessed Virgin Mary, having lost her beloved Son in Jerusalem, sought Him for the space of three days, and at length found Him the fourth day in the Temple, in the midst of the doctors, disputing with them, being then but twelve years old.

Say: One Our Father, Ten Hail Marys, One Glory Be to the Father.

Prayer: Most Blessed Virgin, more than martyr in thy sufferings, and yet the comfort of the afflicted, by. the unspeakable joy which filled thy soul on finding thy beloved Son in the Temple, disputing with the doctors, obtain that we may so effectually seek as to find Him, and never be separated from Him.

I pray for the gift of the virtue of
Piety.

Say: The "Hail, Holy Queen," as on p. 124.

Let Us Pray

O God, whose only-begotten Son, by His life, death, and resurrection, has purchased for us the rewards of eternal life, grant, we beseech Thee, that meditating on these mysteries in the most holy Rosary of the Blessed Virgin Mary, we may imitate what they contain, and obtain what they promise through Christ our Lord.   Amen.

The Sorrowful Mysteries

First Mystery—The Agony of Our Blessed Savior in the Garden

Meditation: Let us contemplate in this mystery how our Blessed Savior was so afflicted for us in the garden of Gethsemani, that His body was bathed in a bloody sweat, which ran trickling down in great drops to the ground.

Say: One Our Father, Ten Hail Marys, One Glory Be to the Father.

Prayer: Most holy Virgin, more than martyr, by that fervent prayer which thy most beloved Son poured forth to His Father in the garden, vouchsafe to intercede for us, that we may always and in all things conform and subject ourselves to the will of God. Amen.

I pray for the gift of the virtue of
Contrition.

Second Mystery—The Scourging of Our Lord at the Pillar

Meditation: Let us contemplate in this mystery how our Lord Jesus Christ was most cruelly scourged by Pilate's order, receiving, as was revealed to St. Bridget, about five thousand stripes.

Say: One Our Father, Ten Hail Marys, One Glory Be to the Father.

Prayer: O Mother of God, overflowing fountain of patience, by the stripes thy beloved Son vouchsafed to endure for us, obtain for us grace to mortify our rebellious senses, and with that sword of grief which pierced thy most tender soul, to cut off all occasions of sin. Amen.

I pray for the gift of the virtue of
Purity.

79

***Third Mystery—The Crowning of Our Savior
with Thorns***

Meditation: Let us contemplate in this mystery
how those cruel ministers of Satan plaited a
crown of sharp thorns, and most cruelly pressed
it on the most sacred head of our Lord Jesus
Christ.

> *Say: One Our Father, Ten Hail Marys, One
> Glory Be to the Father.*

Prayer: O Mother of the eternal King of glory,
by those sharp thorns wherewith his Holy head
was pierced, we beseech thee that by thy intercession we may be delivered here from all mo-
tions of pride and in the day of judgment from
that confusion which our sins deserve.   Amen.

I pray for the gift of the virtue of
Courage.

Fourth Mystery—Jesus Carries His Cross

Meditation: Let us contemplate in this mystery
how our Lord Jesus Christ, being sentenced to
die, bore with great patience the cross which
was laid upon Him for His greater torment and
ignominy.

*Say: One Our Father, Ten Hail Marys, One
Glory Be to the Father.*

Prayer: O Holy Virgin, example of patience, by
the most painful carrying of the cross on which
thy Son, our Lord Jesus Christ, bore the heavy
weight of our sins, obtain of Him for us, by thy
intercession, courage and strength to follow His
steps, and bear our cross after Him to the end
of our lives.   Amen.

I pray for the gift of the virtue of
Patience.

Fifth Mystery—The Crucifixion

Meditation: Let us contemplate in this mystery
how our Lord Jesus Christ, having come to
Mount Calvary, was stripped of His clothes, and
His hands and feet most cruelly nailed to the
cross, in the presence of His most afflicted
Mother.

*Say: One Our Father, Ten Hail Marys, One
Glory Be to the Father.*

Prayer: O Holy Mary, Mother of God, as the
body of thy beloved Son was for us extended on
the cross, so may our desires be daily more and
more stretched out in His service, and our hearts

81

wounded with compassion for His most bitter passion. And thou, O most blessed Virgin, graciously vouchsafe to help us to accomplish the work of our salvation by thy powerful intercession. Amen.

I pray for the gift of the virtue of
Self-Denial.

Say: The "Hail, Holy Queen," as on p. 124.

Let Us Pray

O God, whose only-begotten Son, by His life, death, and resurrection, has purchased for us the rewards of eternal life, grant, we beseech Thee, that meditating on these mysteries in the most holy Rosary of the Blessed Virgin Mary, we may imitate what they contain, and obtain what they promise through Christ our Lord. Amen.

The Glorious Mysteries

First Mystery—The Resurrection

Meditation: Let us contemplate in this mystery how our Lord Jesus Christ, triumphing gloriously over death, rose again the third day, immortal and impassible.

Say: One Our Father, Ten Hail Marys, One Glory Be to the Father.

Prayer: O Glorious Virgin Mary, by the unspeakable joy thou didst feel at the resurrection of thy beloved Son, we beseech thee to obtain that our hearts may never go astray after the false joys of this world, but may be ever and wholly employed in the pursuit of the only true and solid joys of heaven. Amen.

I pray for the gift of the virtue of Faith.

Second Mystery—The Ascension

Meditation: Let us contemplate in this mystery how our Lord Jesus Christ, forty days after His resurrection, ascended into heaven, attended by angels, in the sight of His most holy Mother, His apostles and disciples, to the great admiration of them all.

Say: One Our Father, Ten Hail Marys, One Glory Be to the Father.

Prayer: O Mother of God, comfort of the afflicted, as thy beloved Son, when He ascended into heaven, lifted up His hands and blessed His apostles, so vouchsafe, most holy Mother, to lift up thy pure hands to Him for us, that we may enjoy the benefit of His blessing here on earth, and hereafter in heaven.   Amen.

I pray for the gift of the virtue of
Hope.

Third Mystery—The Descent of the Holy Spirit

Meditation: Let us contemplate in this mystery how our Lord Jesus Christ, being seated on the right hand of God, sent, as He had promised, the Holy Spirit upon the apostles, who, after His ascension, continued in prayer at Jerusalem, in company with the Blessed Virgin, expecting the performance of His promise.

Say: One Our Father, Ten Hail Marys, One Glory Be to the Father.

Prayer: O Blessed Virgin, tabernacle of the Holy Spirit, we beseech thee to obtain that the heavenly Comforter, whom thy beloved Son sent on His apostles to replenish them with spiritual joy, may teach us in this world the true way of salvation, and strengthen us to walk in the path of virtue and good works.   Amen.

I pray for the gift of the virtue of
Love.

Fourth Mystery—The Assumption

Meditation: Let us contemplate in this mystery how the glorious Virgin, twelve years after the resurrection of her Son, passed out of this world unto Him, and was by Him assumed into heaven, accompanied by the holy angels.

Say: One Our Father, Ten Hail Marys, One Glory Be to the Father.

Prayer: O most prudent Virgin, who by thy entrance into the heavenly palace did fill the angels with joy and man with hope, vouchsafe to intercede for us at the hour of death, that, free from the illusions and temptations of the devil, we may joyfully and successfully pass out of this temporal state to enjoy the happiness of eternal life.   Amen.

I pray for the gift of the virtue of
Eternal Happiness.

Fifth Mystery—The Coronation of the Blessed Virgin

Meditation: Let us contemplate in this mystery how the Blessed Virgin Mary was crowned by her Son with the brightest diadem of glory, to the great exultation of the whole court of heaven and the particular triumph of the saints.

*Say: One Our Father, Ten Hail Marys, One
Glory Be to the Father.*

Prayer: O Glorious Queen of all the heavenly
citizens, we beseech thee to accept this Rosary,
which as a crown of roses we lay at thy feet;
and grant, most gracious Lady, that by thy intercession our souls may be inflamed with so
ardent a desire to see thee so gloriously crowned,
that it may never die in us until it be changed
into the happy fruition of thy blessed sight.
Amen.

I pray for the gift of the virtue of
Devotion to Mary.

Say: The "Hail, Holy Queen," as on p. 124.

Let Us Pray

O God, whose only-begotten Son, by His life,
death, and resurrection, has purchased for us
the rewards of eternal life, grant, we beseech
Thee, that meditating on these mysteries in the
most holy Rosary of the Blessed Virgin Mary,
we may imitate what they contain, and obtain
what they promise through Christ our Lord.
Amen.

NOVENA TO ST. ANN

Glorious St. Ann, filled with compassion for those who invoke you, with love for those who suffer, heavily laden with the weight of my troubles, I kneel at your feet and humbly beg of you to take the present affair which I recommend to you under your special protection. (*Here mention request.*) Vouchsafe to recommend it to your daughter, the Blessed Virgin Mary, and lay it before the throne of Jesus. Cease not to intercede for me until my request is granted. Above all, obtain for me the grace of one day beholding my God face to face, and with you and Mary and all the saints praising Him through all eternity.   Amen.

FIRST DAY

Great St. Ann, engrave indelibly on my heart and in my mind the words which have reclaimed and sanctified so many sinners: "What shall it profit a man to gain the whole world if he lose his own soul?" May this be the principal fruit of these exercises by which I will strive to honor you during this Novena. At thy feet I renew my resolution to invoke you daily, not only for the success of my temporal affairs and to be preserved from sickness and suffering, but above all, that I may be preserved from all sin, and that I may succeed in working out my eternal salvation. O most powerful St. Ann, do not let me lose my soul, but obtain for me the grace of winning my way to heaven, there with you, your blessed spouse and your glorious daughter, to sing the praise of the most holy and adorable Trinity forever and ever.   Amen.

Our Father, Hail Mary, and Glory Be to the Father.

Pray for us, St. Ann.
That we may be made worthy of the promises of Christ.

SECOND DAY

Glorious St. Ann, how can you be otherwise than overflowing with tenderness toward sinners like myself, since you are the grandmother of Him who shed His blood for them, and the mother of her whom the saints call the advocate of sinners? To you, therefore, I address my prayers with confidence. Vouchsafe to commend me to Jesus and Mary so that, at your request, they may grant me remission of my sins, perseverance, the love of God, charity for all mankind, and the special grace (*name it*) of

88

which I stand in need at the present time. O most powerful protectress, let me not lose my soul, but obtain for me that, through the merits of Jesus Christ and the intercession of Mary, I may have the happiness of seeing them, of loving and praising them with you for all eternity. Amen.

Our Father, Hail Mary, and Glory Be to the Father.

Pray for us, St. Ann.
That we may be made worthy of the promises of Christ.

THIRD DAY

Beloved of Jesus, Mary and Joseph, mother of the Queen of Heaven, take us and all who are dear to us under thy special care. Obtain for us the virtues thou did instill into the heart of her who was destined to become the Mother of God, and the graces with which thou wast endowed. Sublime model of Christian womanhood, pray that we may imitate your example in our homes and families, listen to our petitions, and obtain our requests. Guardian of the infancy and childhood of the most Blessed Virgin Mary, obtain the graces necessary for all who enter the marriage state, that imitating your virtues they may sanctify their homes and lead the souls

entrusted to their care to eternal glory.   Amen.
Our Father, Hail Mary, and Glory Be to the Father.

Pray for us, St. Ann.
That we may be made worthy of the promises of Christ.

FOURTH DAY

Glorious Saint, I kneel in confidence at your feet, for you also have tasted the bitterness and sorrow of life. My necessities, the cause of my tears, are (*name them*). Good St. Ann, thou who did suffer much during the twenty years that preceded your glorious maternity, I beseech thee, by all your sufferings and humiliations, to grant my prayer. I pray you, through your love for your glorious spouse, through your love for your immaculate child, through the joy you did feel at the moment of her happy birth, not to refuse me. Bless me, bless my family and all who are dear to me, so that some day we may all be with you in the glory of heaven, for all eternity. Amen.

Pray for us, St. Ann.
That we may be made worthy of the promises of Christ.

FIFTH DAY

Great Saint, how far I am from resembling you. I so easily give way to impatience and discouragement; and so easily give up praying when God does not at once grant my request. Prayer is the key to all heavenly treasures and I cannot pray, because my weak faith and languid confidence fail me at the slightest delay of divine mercy. O my powerful protectress, come to my aid; cause my confidence and fervor, supported by the promises of Jesus Christ, to redouble in proportion as the trial to which God in His goodness subjects me is prolonged, that I may thus obtain like you more than I can venture to ask. In the future I will remember that I am made for heaven and not for earth, for eternity and not for time; that consequently I must ask, above all, the salvation of my soul which is assured to all who pray properly and who persevere in prayer.   Amen.

Pray for us, St. Ann.
That we may be made worthy of the promises of Christ.

SIXTH DAY

Glorious St. Ann, mother of the Mother of God, I beg you to obtain through your powerful intercession the pardon of my sins and the assistance I need in my troubles. What can I not hope for if you deign to take me under your protection? The Most High has been pleased to grant the prayers of sinners, whenever you have been charitable enough to be their advocate.

Kneeling at your feet, I beg you to help me in all spiritual and temporal dangers; to guide me in the true path of Christian perfection, and finally to obtain for me the grace of ending my life with the death of the just, so that I may contemplate face to face your beloved Jesus and your daughter Mary in your loving companionship throughout eternity. Amen.

Pray for us, St. Ann.
That we may be made worthy of the promises of Christ.

SEVENTH DAY

O good St. Ann, so justly called the mother of the infirm, the cure of those who suffer from disease, look kindly upon the sick for whom I pray; alleviate their sufferings; cause them to sanctify their sufferings by patience and complete submission to the divine will; finally deign to obtain health for them and with it the firm resolution to honor Jesus, Mary and yourself by the faithful performance of duties. But, merciful St. Ann, I ask you above all, salvation of the soul, rather than bodily health, for I am convinced that this fleeting life is given us solely to assure us a better one. Now, we cannot obtain that better life without the help of God's graces. I earnestly beg them of you for the sick and for myself, through the merits of our Lord Jesus Christ, through the intercession of His Immaculate Mother and through your efficacious and powerful mediation, O glorious St. Ann. Amen.

Pray for us, St. Ann.
That we may be made worthy of the promises of Christ.

EIGHTH DAY

Remember, O St. Ann, you whose name signifies grace and mercy, that never was it known that anyone who fled to your protection, implored your help and sought your intercession was left unaided. Inspired with this confidence, I fly unto you, good and kind mother; I take refuge at your feet and, sinful as I am, I venture to appear before you, groaning under the weight of my sins. O holy mother of the Immaculate Virgin Mary, despise not my petitions but hear me and grant my prayer.   Amen.

Pray for us, St. Ann.

That we may be made worthy of the promises of Christ.

NINTH DAY

Most holy mother of the Virgin Mary, glorious St. Ann, I, a miserable sinner, confiding in your kindness, choose you today as my special advocate. I offer and consecrate my person and all my interests to your care and maternal solicitude. I hope to serve and honor you all my life for the love of your most holy daughter and to do all in my power to spread devotion to you.

O my very good mother and advocate, deign to accept me as your servant and to adopt me as your child. O glorious St. Ann, I beg you, by the passion of my most loving Jesus, the Son of Mary, your most holy daughter, to assist me in all the necessities both of my body and my soul. Venerable Mother, I beg you to obtain for me the grace of leading a life perfectly conformable in all things to the divine will. I place my soul in your hands and in those of your kind daughter. I confide it to you, above all at the moment when it will be about to separate itself from my body in order that, appearing under your patronage before the Supreme Judge, He may find it worthy of enjoying His divine presence in your holy companionship in heaven. Amen.

Pray for us, St. Ann.
That we may be made worthy of the promises of Christ.

Litany in Honor of St. Ann

(*For Private Devotion*)

Lord, have mercy on us.
Christ, have mercy on us.
Lord, have mercy on us.
Christ, hear us.
Christ, graciously hear us.
God the Father of Heaven,
have mercy on us.
God the Son, Redeemer of the world, *have mercy on us.*
God the Holy Spirit, *have mercy on us.*
Holy Trinity, one God, *have mercy on us.*

St. Ann,*
St. Ann, Mother of the Virgin Mary,
St. Ann, Spouse of St. Joachim,
St. Ann, Ark of Noah,
St. Ann, Ark of the Covenant,
St. Ann, Joy of Angels,
St. Ann, Grace of patriarchs,
St. Ann, Oracle of Prophets,
St. Ann, Praise of All Saints,
St. Ann, Mirror of Obedience,
St. Ann, Mirror of Patience,
St. Ann, Mirror of Compassion,
St. Ann, Mirror of Devotion,
St. Ann, Mirror of Piety,
St. Ann, Bulwark of the Church,
St. Ann, Deliverer of Captives,
St. Ann, Mother of Widows,
St. Ann, Mother of Virgins,
St. Ann, Mother of the Sick,
St. Ann, Light of the Blind,
St. Ann, Tongue of the Dumb,
St. Ann, Hearing of the Deaf,
St. Ann, Comforter of the Afflicted,
St. Ann, never invoked without answer,

Lamb of God, who take away the sins of the world, *spare us, O Lord.*

* *Pray for us.*

95

Lamb of God, who take away the sins of the world, *graciously hear us, O Lord.*

Lamb of God, who take away the sins of the world, *have mercy on us.*

Pray for us, St. Ann.

That we may be made worthy of the promises of Christ.

Let Us Pray

O God, who did vouchsafe to endow Blessed St. Ann with grace that she was found worthy to be the mother of her who brought forth Your only-begotten Son, grant in Thy grace, that we who devoutly honor her memory, may through her prayers attain everlasting life, through Jesus Christ our Lord. Amen.

NOVENA TO ST. ANTHONY

Novena Prayer to St. Anthony

O wonderful St. Anthony, glorious on account of the fame of thy miracles, and through the condescension of Jesus in coming in the form of a little child to rest in thy arms, obtain for me of His bounty the grace which I ardently desire from the depths of my heart . . . Thou who was so compassionate toward miserable sinners, regard not the unworthiness of those who pray to thee, but the glory of God that it may be once again magnified by the particular request which I now ask for with persevering earnestness.

One Our Father, one Hail Mary and one Glory Be to the Father, in honor of St. Anthony.

FIRST DAY

O holy St. Anthony, gentlest of saints, your love for God and charity for His creatures made you worthy while on earth to possess miraculous powers. Miracles waited on your word, which you were ever ready to speak for those in trouble or anxiety. Encouraged by this thought, I implore you to obtain for me the favor I seek in this novena. . . . The answer to my prayer may require a miracle; even so, you are the saint of miracles. O gentle and loving St. Anthony, whose heart was ever full of human sympathy, whisper my petition into the ears of the Infant Jesus, who loved to be folded in your arms, and the gratitude of my heart will always be yours.

St. Anthony, pray for us.

SECOND DAY

O miracle-working St. Anthony, remember that it never has been heard that thou hast left without help or relief anyone who in his need had recourse to thee. Animated now with the most lively confidence, even with full conviction of not being refused, I fly for refuge to thee, O most favored friend of the Infant Jesus. O eloquent preacher of the divine mercy, despise not my supplications but, bringing them before the throne of God, strengthen them by thy intercession and obtain for me the favor I seek in this novena . . .

St. Anthony, pray for us.

THIRD DAY

O purest St. Anthony, who through thy angelic virtue was made worthy to be caressed by the

Divine Child Jesus, to hold Him in thy arms and press Him to thy heart, I entreat thee to cast a benevolent glance upon me. O glorious St. Anthony, born under the protection of Mary Immaculate, on the Feast of her Assumption into heaven, and consecrated to her and now so powerful an intercessor in heaven, we beseech thee, obtain for us the favor we ask in this novena. . . . O great wonder-worker, intercede for us that God may grant us our request.

St. Anthony, pray for us.

FOURTH DAY

We salute and honor thee, O powerful helper, St. Anthony. The Christian world confidently turns to thee and experiences thy tender compassion and powerful assistance in so many necessities and sufferings that we are encouraged in our need to seek thy help in obtaining a favorable answer to our request for the favor we seek in this novena. . . . O holy St. Anthony, we beseech thee, obtain for us the grace that we desire.

St. Anthony, pray for us.

FIFTH DAY

We salute thee, St. Anthony, lily of purity, ornament and glory of Christianity. We salute thee, great Saint, cherub of wisdom and seraph of divine love. We rejoice at the favors our Lord has so liberally bestowed on thee. In humility and confidence we entreat thee to help us, for we know that God has given thee charity and pity, as well as power. We ask thee by the love thou didst feel toward the Infant Jesus as thou held him in thy arms to tell him now of the favor we seek through your intercession in this novena . . .

St. Anthony, pray for us.

SIXTH DAY

O glorious St. Anthony, chosen by God to preach His Word, thou didst receive from Him the gift of tongues and the power of working the most extraordinary miracles. O good St. Anthony, pray that I may fulfill the will of God in all things so that I may love Him, with thee, for all eternity. O kind St. Anthony, we beseech thee, obtain for us the grace that we desire, the favor we seek in this novena . . .

St. Anthony, pray for us.

SEVENTH DAY

O renowned champion of the faith of Christ, most holy St. Anthony, glorious for your many miracles, obtain for me from the bounty of my Lord and God the grace which I ardently seek in this novena . . . O holy St. Anthony, ever attentive to those who invoke thee, grant us the aid of thy powerful intercession.

St. Anthony, pray for us.

EIGHTH DAY

O holy St. Anthony, thou hast shown thyself so powerful in thy intercession, so tender and so compassionate toward those who honor thee and invoke thee in suffering and distress. I beseech thee most humbly and earnestly to take me under thy protection in my present necessities and to obtain for me the favor I desire . . . Vouchsafe to recommend my request to the merciful Queen of heaven, that she may plead my cause with you before the throne of her Divine Son.

St. Anthony, pray for us.

NINTH DAY

St. Anthony, servant of Mary, glory of the Church, pray for our Holy Father, our bishops, our priests, our Religious Orders, that, through their pious zeal and apostolic labors, all may be united in faith and give greater glory to God. St. Anthony, helper of all who invoke you, pray for me and intercede for me before the throne of Almighty God that I be granted the favor I so earnestly seek in this novena . . .

St. Anthony, pray for us.

May the divine assistance remain always with us.   Amen.

May the souls of the faithful departed, through the mercy of God, rest in peace.   Amen.

O God, may the votive commemoration of the blessed Anthony, Thy confessor, be a source of joy to Thy Church, that she may always be fortified with spiritual assistance, and deserve to enjoy eternal rewards. Through Christ our Lord. Amen.

Litany of St. Anthony

Lord, have mercy on us.
Christ, have mercy on us.
Lord, have mercy on us.
Christ, hear us.
Christ, graciously hear us.

Holy Mary,*
St. Anthony of Padua,
St. Anthony, martyr in desiring to die for Christ,
St. Anthony, pillar of the Church,
St. Anthony, worthy priest of God,
St. Anthony, apostolic preacher,
St. Anthony, teacher of truth,
St. Anthony, hammer of heretics,
St. Anthony, comforter of the afflicted,

St. Anthony, helper in necessities,
St. Anthony, deliverer of captives,
St. Anthony, guide of the erring,
St. Anthony, restorer of lost things,
St. Anthony, chosen intercessor,
St. Anthony, continuous worker of miracles,
Be merciful unto us, spare us, O Lord.
Be merciful unto us, graciously hear us, O Lord.
From all evil,
   O Lord, deliver us.
From all sin,
From all dangers of body and soul,
From the snares of the devil,

* *Pray for us.*

102

From pestilence, famine and war,*
From eternal death,
Through the merits of St. Anthony,
Through his zeal for the conversion of sinners,
Through his desire for the crown of martyrdom,
Through his fatigues and teaching,
Through his penitential tears,
Through his patience and humility,
Through his glorious death,
Through the number of his prodigies,
In the day of judgment,
We sinners,**
That Thou wouldst vouchsafe to bring us to true penance,
That Thou wouldst vouchsafe to assist us in our necessities,
That Thou wouldst vouchsafe to grant our petitions,
That Thou wouldst vouchsafe to kindle the fire of divine love within us,
That Thou wouldst vouchsafe us the protection and intercession of St. Anthony,
Son of God,

Lamb of God, who take away the sins of the world, *spare us, O Lord.*
Lamb of God, who take away the sins of the world, *graciously hear us, O Lord.*
Lamb of God, who take away the sins of the world, *have mercy on us.*
Christ, hear us.
Christ, graciously hear us.
Pray for us, St. Anthony.
That we may be made worthy of the promises of Christ.

* *Pray for us.*
** *We beseech Thee, hear us.*

NOVENA TO THE LITTLE FLOWER

O St. Theresa of the Child Jesus, who during your short life on earth became a mirror of angelic purity, of love strong as death, and of wholehearted abandonment to God, now that you rejoice in the reward of your virtues, cast a glance of pity on me as I leave all things in your hands. Make my troubles your own, speak a word for me to our Lady Immaculate, whose flower of special love you were—to that Queen of Heaven "who smiled on you at the dawn of life." Beg her as Queen of the heart of Jesus to obtain for me by her powerful intercession the grace I yearn for so ardently at this moment . . . and that she join with it a blessing that may strengthen me during life, defend me at the hour of death, and lead me straight on to a happy eternity.   Amen.

O God, who did inflame with Thy Spirit of Love, the soul of Thy servant, Therese of the Child Jesus, grant that we also may love Thee and make Thee much loved.   Amen.

FIRST DAY

O Theresa of the Child Jesus, well beloved and full of charity, in union with you, I reverently adore the Majesty of God; and since I rejoice with exceeding joy in the singular gifts of grace bestowed upon you during your life, and your gifts of glory after death, I give Him deepest thanks for them; I beseech you with all my heart's devotion to be pleased to obtain for me, by your effectual intercession, above all things, the grace of a holy life and a happy death. Moreover, I beg of you to obtain for me . . . But if what I ask of you so earnestly does not tend to the glory of God and the greater good of my soul, do you, I pray, obtain for me that which is more profitable to both these ends. Amen.

St. Theresa of the Child Jesus, pray for us.

SECOND DAY

Almighty God, giver of all good gifts, who did will that Blessed Theresa, being watered by the heavenly dew of your guiding grace, should bloom in Carmel with the beauty of virginity and patience in suffering, grant that we your servants may go forward in the order of her sweetness and may be found worthy to become devoted and loyal followers of Christ. Amen.

St. Theresa of the Child Jesus, pray for us.

THIRD DAY

O St. Theresa of the Child Jesus, lily of purity, ornament and glory of Carmel, I greet you, great

105

saint, seraph of divine love. I rejoice in the favors our Lord so liberally bestowed on you. In humility and confidence I ask you to help me, for I know that God has given you love and pity as well as power. Tell Him, now, I beseech you, of the favor I seek in this novena . . . Your request will crown my petition with success and bring joy to my heart. Remember your promise to do good on earth: "I shall spend my heaven doing good on earth. After death I shall let fall a shower of roses."

St. Theresa of the Child Jesus, pray for us.

FOURTH DAY

O Little Flower of Jesus, who at an early age had your heart set on Carmel and in your brief earthly life did become a mirror of angelic purity, of courageous love and of whole-hearted surrender to Almighty God, turn your eyes of mercy upon us who trust in you. Obtain for us the favor we seek in this novena . . . and the grace to keep our hearts and minds pure and clean. O dear saint, grant us to feel in every need the power of your intercession; help to comfort us in all the bitterness of this life and especially at its end, that we may be worthy to share eternal happiness with you in heaven. Amen.

St. Theresa of the Child Jesus, pray for us.

FIFTH DAY

O Little Flower of Carmel, Almighty God endowed you, consumed by love for Him, with wondrous spiritual strength to follow the way of perfection during the days of your short life. Sickness touched you early but you remained firm in faith and prayer was your life. O pray for me that I may benefit by your intercession and be granted the favor I ask in this novena . . .

St. Theresa of the Child Jesus, pray for us.

SIXTH DAY

O Little Flower of Jesus, you have shown yourself so powerful in your intercession, so tender and compassionate toward those who honor you and invoke you in suffering and distress, that I kneel at your feet with perfect confidence and beseech you most humbly and earnestly to take me under your protection in my present necessity and to obtain for me the favor I ask in this novena . . . Vouchsafe to recommend my request to Mary, the merciful Queen of Heaven, that she may plead my cause with you before the throne of Jesus, her divine Son. Cease not to intercede for me until my request is granted.

St. Theresa of the Child Jesus, pray for us.

SEVENTH DAY

Theresa of the Child Jesus, most loving saint, in union with you I adore the divine Majesty. My heart is filled with joy at the remembrance of the marvelous favors with which God blessed your life on earth and of the great glory that came to you after death. In union with you, I praise God, and offer Him my humble tribute of thanksgiving. I implore you to obtain for me, through your powerful intercession, the greatest of all blessings—that of living and dying in the state of grace. I also beg of you to secure for me the special favor I seek in this novena . . .

St. Theresa of the Child Jesus, pray for us.

EIGHTH DAY

O glorious St. Theresa, who, burning with the desire of increasing the glory of God, invariably attended to the sanctification of your own soul by the constant practice of prayer and charity so that, becoming in the Church a model of holiness, you are now in heaven the protector of all those who have recourse to you in faith, look down upon us who invoke your powerful patronage and join your petition to ours that we be granted the favor we seek in this novena . . .

St. Theresa of the Child Jesus, pray for us.

NINTH DAY

O St. Theresa, seraphic virgin, beloved spouse of our crucified Lord, you who on earth did burn with a love so intense toward your God and my God, and now glow with a bright and purer flame in paradise, obtain for me, I beseech you, a spark of that same holy fire which shall help me to put the things of the world in their proper place and live my life always conscious of the presence of the God. As I conclude my novena I also beg of you to secure for me the special favor I seek at this time . . .

St. Theresa of the Child Jesus, pray for us.

Litany of the Little Flower of Jesus

Lord, have mercy on us.
Christ, have mercy on us.
Lord, have mercy on us.
Christ, hear us.
Christ, graciously hear us.
God the Father of Heaven, *have mercy on us.*
God the Son, Redeemer of the world, *have mercy on us.*
God the Holy Spirit, *have mercy on us.*
Holy Trinity, one God, *have mercy on us.*

Holy Mary,*
Our Lady of Victory,
Little Therese, servant of God,

Little Therese, victim of the merciful love of God,
Little Therese, spouse of Jesus,
Little Therese, gift of Heaven,
Little Therese, remarkable in childhood,
Little Therese, an example of obedience,
Little Therese, resigned to the Divine Will of God,
Little Therese, lover of peace,
Little Therese, lover of patience,
Little Therese, lover of gentleness,

* *Pray for us.*

109

Little Therese, heroic in sacrifices,*

Little Therese, generous in forgiving,

Little Therese, benefactress of the needy,

Little Therese, lover of Jesus,

Little Therese, devoted to the Holy Face,

Little Therese, consumed with Divine love of God,

Little Therese, advocate of extreme cases,

Little Therese, persevering in prayer,

Little Therese, a powerful advocate with God,

Little Therese, showering roses,

Little Therese, doing good upon earth,

Little Therese, answering all prayers,

Little Therese, lover of holy chastity,

Little Therese, lover of voluntary poverty,

Little Therese, lover of obedience,

Little Therese, burning with zeal for God's glory,

Little Therese, inflamed with the spirit of love,

Little Therese, child of benediction,

Little Therese, perfect in simplicity,

Little Therese, so remarkable for trust in God,

Little Therese, gifted with unusual intelligence,

Little Therese, never invoked without some answer,

Little Therese, teaching us the sure way,

Little Therese, victim of Divine Love,

Lamb of God, who take away the sins of the world, *spare us, O Lord.*

Lamb of God, who take away the sins of the world, *graciously hear us, O Lord.*

Lamb of God, who take away the sins of the world, *have mercy on us.*

Little Flower of Jesus, pray for us.

* *Pray for us.*

Without a
Divinity there
is for man
neither purpose,
Goal, nor hope,
only a
trembling future,
an eternal fear
of the dark.

Jean Paul

General
Prayers

THE HOLY ROSARY

The Rosary is a devotion to the Incarnation of Our Lord and to His Blessed Mother. It is composed of fifteen decades, each decade consisting of the Our Father, ten Hail Marys, and the Glory Be to the Father, and each being recited in honor of some mystery in the life of Our Lord and of His Blessed Mother. During each decade we should call to mind the mystery which it is intended to honor, and pray that we may learn to practice the virtue specially taught us by that mystery.

I—The Five Joyful Mysteries

1. The Annunciation
2. The Visitation
3. The Nativity
4. The Presentation
5. The Finding in the Temple

II—The Five Sorrowful Mysteries

1. The Agony in the Garden
2. The Scourging at the Pillar

3. The Crowning with Thorns
4. The Carrying of the Cross
5. The Crucifixion

III—*The Five Glorious Mysteries*

1. The Resurrection
2. The Ascension
3. The Coming of the Holy Spirit on the Apostles
4. The Assumption of the Blessed Virgin
5. The Coronation of the Blessed Virgin

THE WAY OF THE CROSS

Preparatory Prayer

O Lord, at this time I want to think of your journey to Calvary. You went along this way out of obedience to the Father and out of love for me. You took upon yourself the heavy cross to atone for my sins and to redeem the world. In these thoughts on your passion let me be grateful for so great a love. Mary, Mother of Sorrows, accompany me along this way.

1. *Jesus Is Condemned to Death*

Thy will, O God is supreme. May my one great purpose be to seek it and to follow it.

2. *Jesus Receives the Cross*

Grant, O divine Savior, that I may faithfully fulfill every duty for love of Thee.

3. *Jesus Falls the First Time under the Cross*

How many times, O Lord, have I been faithless through sin to Thee.

4. *Jesus Is Met by His Blessed Mother*

Mary, my mother, intercede for me with thy Divine Son.

5. *The Cross Is Laid Upon Simon of Cyrene*

Every time I put temptation aside and resist sin, I help Thee, Jesus, to carry Thy cross.

6. *Veronica Wipes the Face of Jesus*

Thy suffering was for me. I will not desert Thee, but always defend Thee.

7. *Jesus Falls the Second Time*

Forgive me, O merciful Lord, my many, my repeated sins.

8. *Jesus Speaks to the Women of Jerusalem*

Thy words of mercy and pardon give me fresh hope and confidence.

9. *Jesus Falls the Third Time*

May my sins never discourage me, but lead me to seek more and more Thy help.

10. *Jesus Is Stripped of His Garments*

I will be Thy valiant follower. May my conduct never shame Thee before men.

11. *Jesus Is Nailed to the Cross*

Thy commands mean that I should conquer every unholy desire. I will conquer in Thy name.

12. *Jesus Dies on the Cross*

When my hour comes, may I die bravely, dear Jesus, for Thee.

13. *Jesus Is Taken Down from the Cross*

Wherever I am, Thou, O Lord, will be my true, though unseen companion.

14. *Jesus Is Laid in the Sepulchre*

Thee, my eternal God, will I always serve. With Thee I live, and with Thee I die.

Prayers for Special Occasions

Prayer for Light

O Holy Spirit of God, take me as Thy disciple: guide me, illuminate me, sanctify me. Bind my hands that they may do no evil; cover my eyes that they may see it no more; sanctify my heart that evil may not dwell within me. Be Thou my God; be Thou my guide. Wherever You lead me I will go; whatever You forbid me I will renounce; and whatever You command me in Thy strength I will do. Lead me, then, unto the fullness of Your truth.   Amen.

Prayer for All in Trouble

Most blessed Virgin, in your life of glory, remember the sorrows of earth. Look with kindness on those who suffer, who struggle against difficulties, who drink unceasingly the bitterness of this life. Have pity on those who love each other and are separated. Have pity on the lonely of heart. Have pity on the weakness of our faith. Have pity on the objects of our affection. Have pity on those who weep, those who pray, those

who fear. Obtain for all, hope and peace.
Amen.

Act of Spiritual Communion

My Jesus, I believe in Thee; I hope in Thee;
I love Thee. I am heartily sorry for all my sins.
Come into my heart, cleanse it, purify it, and
remain there forever. My Lord, Jesus Christ,
preserve my soul unto life everlasting.

For Our Own Beloved Dead

Good Jesus, whose loving Heart was ever
troubled by the sorrows of others, look with
pity on the souls of our dear ones in purgatory.
O You, who "loved Your own," hear our cry
for mercy, and grant that those whom You
called from our homes and hearts, may soon
enjoy everlasting rest in the home of Thy love
in heaven. Eternal rest, grant unto them, O
Lord, and let perpetual light shine on them. May
their souls and the souls of all the faithful departed, through the mercy of God, rest in peace.
Amen.

Prayer before the Crucifix

Look down upon me, good and gentle Jesus,
while before Thy face I humbly kneel, and

with burning soul, pray and beseech You to fix deep in my heart lively sentiments of faith, hope and charity, true contrition for my sins, and a firm purpose of amendment; while I contemplate, with great love and tender pity, Thy five most precious wounds, pondering over them within me, calling to mind the words which David, Thy Prophet, said of Thee, my Jesus: "They have pierced My hands and My feet, they have numbered all My bones."

Prayer after Holy Communion

My God, enable me to bear Thee, for Thou alone canst. Cleanse my heart and mind from all that is past. Wipe out clean all my recollections of evil. Rid me from all langor, sickness, irritability, feebleness of soul. Give me a true perception of things unseen, and make me truly, practically, and in the details of my life, prefer Thee to anything on earth, and the future world to the present. Give me a true instinct determining between right and wrong, humility in all things, and a tender, longing love for Thee. (Cardinal Newman)

Prayer in Affliction

O Lord, keep me from bitterness. It is so easy to nurse sharp bitter thoughts each dull dark hour! Against self-pity, Man of Sorrows, defend me with Thy deep understanding and Thy gentle power! And out of all this hurt of pain and heartbreak help me to harvest a new sympathy for suffering humankind; a wiser pity for those who lift a heavier cross with Thee.

Salve Regina

Hail! Holy Queen, Mother of mercy, our life, our sweetness, and our hope! To thee do we cry, poor banished children of Eve; to thee do we send up our sighs, mourning and weeping in this valley of tears. Turn then, most gracious advocate, thine eyes of mercy toward us, and after this our exile show unto us the blessed Fruit of thy womb, Jesus. O clement, O loving, O sweet Virgin Mary; pray for us, O holy Mother of God, that we may be made worthy of the promises of Christ.   Amen.

Prayer for Priests

O Jesus, Eternal Priest, keep Thy priests within the shelter of Thy Sacred Heart, where none may touch them. Keep unstained their anointed hands, which daily touch Thy Sacred Body. Keep unsullied their lips, daily purpled with Thy Precious Blood. Keep pure and unworldly their hearts sealed with the sublime mark of the priesthood. Let Thy holy love surround them from the world's contagion. Bless their labors with abundant fruit, and may the souls to whom they minister be their joy and consolation here and their everlasting crown hereafter. Mary, Queen of the Clergy, pray for us; obtain for us numerous and holy priests.

Prayer for a Happy Death

O God, who has doomed all men to die, but has concealed from all the hour of their death, grant that I may pass my days in the practice of holiness and justice, and that I may deserve to quit this world in the peace of a good conscience, and in the embrace of Thy love. Through the same Christ our Lord. Amen.

Prayer for All in Military Service

O God, we beseech Thee, watch over the souls of all who are exposed to the horrors of war, and to the spiritual dangers inseparable from a military life. Bless them with such a strong faith that no human respect may ever lead them to deny it, or fear to practice it. Do Thou by Thy grace fortify them against the contagion of bad example. Keep them always in Thy friendship. May nothing in life or death ever separate them from Thee. Amen.

Let Me Bring Love

O God, make me an instrument of peace,
that I may bring love where there is hate;
that I may pardon where there is guilt;
that I may unite where there is dissension;
that I may bring truth where there is error;
that I may bring faith where there is darkness;
that I may bring joy where there is suffering;
not to be comforted, but to bring comfort;
not to be understood, but to understand;
not to be loved, but to love; this alone is
   important.
For when we give, we receive;
when we pardon, we are forgiven;
when we die, we enter new life.

Prayer for Enlightenment

Come, Holy Spirit, enlighten the darkness of
my understanding and sharpen my conscience,
so that I may recognize God's will in all things.
Send forth your light and truth into my soul!
May I see all my sins and failures in this light
and confess them with a contrite heart. Jesus
Christ, gentle Savior, I put my hope of salvation
in you. Accept my confession with loving mercy
and move my heart to true sorrow for my sins.
Heavenly Father, when you look into my soul,
look not so much at the evil I have done but at
the genuine sorrow which I feel within my heart.

Help me to confess all my sins with a childlike trust in your loving forgiveness. Amen.

Prayer for the Souls in Purgatory

O Divine Heart of Jesus, grant, we beseech Thee, eternal rest to the souls in purgatory, the final grace to those who shall die today, true repentance to sinners, the light of Faith to pagans, and Thy blessing to me and mine. To Thee, O most compassionate Heart of Jesus, I commend all these souls, and I offer to Thee on their behalf all the merits, together with the merits of Thy most Holy Mother and of all the saints and angels, and all the sacrifices of the Holy Mass, Communions, prayers and good works, which shall be accomplished today throughout the Christian world. Amen.

Act of Resignation

My Lord God, even now resignedly and willingly, I accept at Thy hands with all its anxieties, pains and sufferings whatever kind of death it may please Thee to be mine.

Ejaculations

O Lord, be merciful to me, a sinner.

Lord, increase our faith.

My Jesus, mercy!

O Jesus, friend of the little ones, bless the children of the whole world.

Dear Jesus, hear my prayers and pour the abundance of your graces on those I love.

Heart of Jesus, once in agony, have mercy on the dying.

Heart of Jesus, I place my trust in Thee; for though I fear all things from my weakness, I hope for all things from Thy mercy.

The Divine Praises

Blessed be God!
Blessed be his Holy Name!
Blessed be Jesus Christ, true God and true Man!
Blessed be the name of Jesus!
Blessed be His most Sacred Heart!
Blessed be His most Precious Blood!
Blessed be Jesus in the most holy Sacrament of the Altar!
Blessed be the Holy Spirit, the Paraclete!
Blessed be the great Mother of God, Mary most holy!

Blessed be her holy and Immaculate Conception!
Blessed be her Glorious Assumption!
Blessed be the name of Mary, Virgin and
 Mother!
Blessed be St. Joseph, her most chaste spouse!
Blessed be God in His angels and in His saints!

From the Scriptures

For everything there is a season,
     and a time for every matter under heaven:
A time to be born, and a time to die;
A time to plant, and a time to pluck up what is
     planted;
A time to kill, and a time to heal;
A time to break down, and a time to build up,
A time to weep, and a time to laugh;
A time to mourn, and a time to dance;
A time to cast away stones, and a time to gather
     stones together;
A time to embrace, and a time to refrain from
     embracing;
A time to seek, and a time to lose;
A time to keep, and a time to cast away;
A time to read, and a time to sew;
A time to keep silent, and a time to speak;
A time to love, and a time to hate;
A time for war, and a time for peace.
What gain has the worker from his toil?

Ecclesiastes 3

Train up a child in the way he should go,
and when he is old he will not depart from it.

Proverbs 21

To thee, O God of my fathers,
I give thanks and praise.

Daniel 2

How great are his signs,
how mighty his wonders!
His kingdom is an everlasting kingdom,
and his dominion is from generation to
generation.

Daniel 4

From the Psalms

The Lord is my shepherd, I shall not want;
he makes me lie down in green pastures.
He leads me beside still waters;
he restores my soul.
He guides me in paths of righteousness
for his name's sake.

Even though I walk through the valley of the
shadow of death,

130

I fear no evil;
for you are with me;
    your rod and your staff,
    they comfort me.

You prepare a table before me
    in the presence of my enemies;
You anoint my head with oil,
    my cup overflows.
Surely goodness and mercy shall follow me
    all the days of my life;
and I shall dwell in the house of the Lord
    forever.

Psalm 23

Let my heart rejoice in your salvation;
    let me sing of the Lord,
"He has been good to me."

Psalm 12

Hear, O God, my cry;
    listen to my prayer!
From the earth's end I call to you
    as my heart grows faint.

Psalm 60

Hear my prayer, O Lord;
    let my cry come to thee!
Do not hide thy face from me
    in the day of my distress!
Incline thy ear to me;
    answer me speedily on the day when I call!

Psalm 102

I will give thanks to the Lord with my whole
       heart;
    I will tell of all thy wonderful deeds.
I will be glad and exult in thee,
    I will sing praise to thy name, O Most High.

Psalm 9

To thee, O Lord, I lift up my soul,
    O my God, in thee I trust.

Psalm 25

The Lord is my light and my salvation;
    whom shall I fear?
The Lord is the stronghold of my life;
    of whom shall I be afraid?

Psalm 27

O Lord, our Lord,
how majestic is thy name in all the earth!

Psalm 7

May God be gracious to us and bless us
and make his face to shine upon us.

Psalm 67

Let the words of my mouth and the meditations
of my heart
be acceptable in thy sight,
O Lord, my rock and my redeemer.

Psalm 19

Bless the Lord, O my soul!
O Lord, my God, you are great indeed!

Psalm 103

Probe me, O God, and know my heart;
try me, and know my thoughts;
See if my way is crooked,
and lead me in the way of old.

When I call, answer me, O my good God,
   you who relieve me when I am in distress;
Have pity on me, and hear my prayer!

Psalm 4